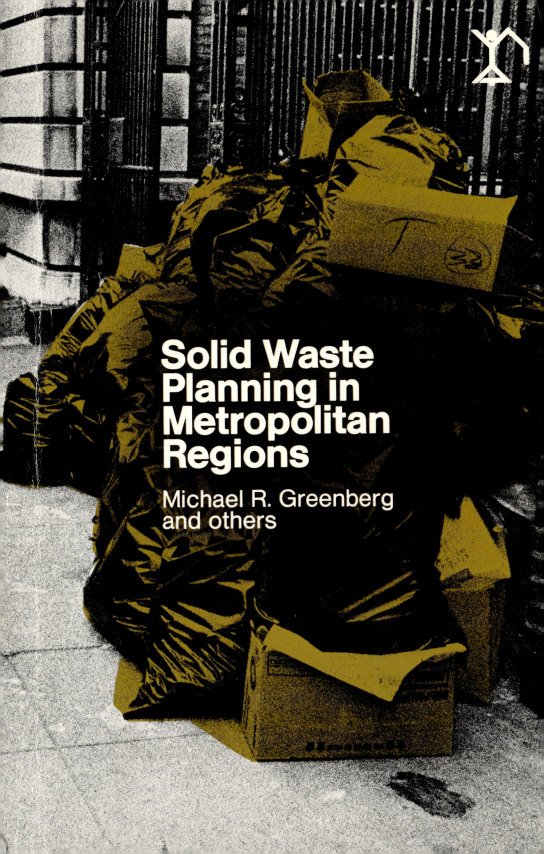

Solid Waste Planning in Metropolitan Regions

Michael R. Greenberg
and others

Solid Waste Planning in Metropolitan Regions

Michael R. Greenberg

and
Mike Bottge
John Caruana
David Horowitz
Beth Krugman
Nicholas Masucci
Anne Milewski
Lester Nebenzahl
Theodore O'Neill
John Skypeck
Nicholas Valente

CENTER
FOR URBAN
POLICY RESEARCH

The Center for Urban Policy Research
Rutgers University
Building 4051–Kilmer Campus
New Brunswick, New Jersey 08903

CONTENTS

ACKNOWLEDGMENTS

The publication of this study was made possible through funds from the Center for Urban Policy Research of Rutgers University. Special thanks are also due to Donna Krabbe of the Office of Solid Waste Management Programs of the United States Environmental Protection Agency and to Edgar Berman of Mitre Corporation for providing one of the nonlinear mathematical models which was tested. Thanks are given to members of the staffs of the New Jersey Department of Environmental Protection, the New Jersey Department of Transportation, and to the many county and local officials who provided us with data and their expertise. Many of these people are acknowledged in the course of the text.

This book represents the combined efforts of one faculty member and ten students from the departments of Urban Planning and Policy Development, Community Development, and Geography of Rutgers University. The project originated in a conversation between Ted O'Neill and myself. From the time of that conversation it took almost a year and a half to complete the study. The research involved hundreds of man-hours and the closest cooperation among a group of students that I have witnessed.

All members of the research group were involved in all sections of the study. We held weekly, and frequently twice-weekly, meetings and all members of the research group participated in the modeling efforts. Nevertheless, the following major responsibilities may be distinguished.

John Caruana was responsible for all the computer-run decks which varied from several hundred cards to seven boxes.

John prepared the initial draft of Chapter 3 on the mathematical model.

David Horowitz, Nicholas Masucci, and Nicholas Valente had the unenviable task of estimating the region's solid waste generation. This involved estimating the region's population and rates of per-capita waste generation. They prepared an initial draft of Chapter 4 on solid waste generation.

Beth Krugman, Lester Nebenzahl, and John Skypeck had the tedious job of calculating the transportation costs between all the waste sources, intermediate facilities, and final sites. Beth prepared an initial draft of a major portion of Chapter 5, which deals with transportation.

Theodore O'Neill, Mick Bottge, and Anne Milewski were responsible for examining the economics of solid waste technologies. Mick prepared an initial draft of a portion of Chapter 7 which focuses on alternative technologies. Anne wrote the initial draft of the Sixth chapter, which deals with the market for recovered waste products. Ted prepared an initial draft of Chapter 7 on alternative technologies, and developed data used to estimate the ton-per-minute costs of moving the region's wastes. In addition, without the benefit of Ted's intuitive knowledge of New Jersey's solid waste system, this project undoubtedly would have been relegated to an academic exercise in modeling.

Michael Greenberg turned the region's solid waste management problem into a mathematical programming problem and directed the research project. He prepared chapters 1, 2, and 8 and the final versions of the remainder of the volume.

Michael R. Greenberg
New Brunswick, New Jersey
December 1975

CHAPTER 1

SUMMARY OF FINDINGS

Solid waste is one of the few readily available and
untapped resources present in urban regions. Once it has
been collected it can be landfilled or reused. Landfilling
entails high economic and environmental costs. In densely
developed urban areas it has been a luxury which is rapidly
being withdrawn from the land-use market. Reuse technologies vary from the well known -- recycling and incineration -- to the relatively new -- dry fuel and pyrolysis.

Our objective was to discover how this potential resource is being used and how it can be used in the future
in northern New Jersey. Specifically, we have constructed
a mathematical model which measures the economic costs of
transporting and processing solid waste given conventional
and new solid waste technologies. We were guided to the
study area by the fact that this region of 3.5 million people has run out of inexpensive landfill options and is
being forced to consider the efficacy of the recovery technologies. The major findings of each chapter are summarized below.

1. The second chapter describes the nation's and the
region's solid waste problems. In the last decade the solid
waste management programs of urban areas have been disrupted
by decreasing availability of inexpensive and conventional
landfill alternatives. The New York region and especially
northern New Jersey face an acute management problem.
Plans and policy decisions have been made to eliminate inexpensive disposal in the Hackensack Meadowlands by 1977.
Currently 45,000 tons of waste are landfilled in the Meadowlands by over 100 communities containing 3.5 million people.
Conventional landfilling alternatives to the Meadowlands
are also rapidly being eliminated.

2. The third chapter reviews one linear and two non-linear programming models used to test the management alternatives. Only the linear model yielded usable results. The model seeks to minimize total regional cost of waste management subject to the constraints that all the waste must be processed and/or disposed of and no facility may receive more waste than it can process or landfill.

3. Chapter 4 estimates the region's solid waste generation at 46,000 tons per week in 1975; 53,000 in 1980; 60,000 in 1985. The distribution of waste loads is prepared for 25 waste sheds from independent projections of population and per-capita solid waste generation.

4. The fifth chapter details the methods used to estimate the costs of moving waste over 319 source-to-facility paths. Independent analyses were made of intraregional truck travel times and of the costs of moving waste by direct haul and with transfer stations.

5. The sixth chapter reviews the potential revenues that can be credited to solid waste as a source of ferrous metal, paper, glass, aluminum, and other nonferrous metals. This analysis discloses that the recovery market is unstable and that only ferrous metal recovery should be credited with limited revenues in planning a recovery system at this time.

6. Chapter 7 reviews alternative processing and disposal technologies: landfilling, incineration, dry fuel, gas and oil pyrolysis, and a total resource recovery system. Cost estimates are derived for these technologies at different operating capacities. On the basis of this analysis and the revenue picture described in chapters 6 and 7, landfilling, dry fuel, and gas pyrolysis are selected as the reasonable technological alternatives to be included in the model.

7. The eighth chapter describes the more than 50 mathematical programming tests which led us to the following policy recommendations. The dry fuel technology demonstrates a clear superiority over any of the alternatives. At best it will produce a net system revenue, irrespective of whether the facilities are concentrated at a central site or dispersed throughout the region. Even with low revenue for the dry fuel product, it is still superior to landfilling alternatives. Given best-and medium-revenue credits for the fuel, gas pyrolysis is a more economical system than landfilling. A dispersed landfill system is slightly more economical than the gas pyrolysis technology if only minimal revenues can be secured for the pyrolysis fuel product. A set of new, dispersed landfill sites offers a slightly less expensive alternative to continued landfilling in the Meadowlands at higher prices. If, as expected, disposal prices in the Meadowlands rise in order to finance a shredding and

baling system, and other alternatives are not provided, the region's solid waste management costs would at least double.

In conclusion, the public attitude toward solid waste has been that it simply wants the waste to go to the cheapest disposal site. However, the disposal of erstwhile trash without endangering public health and with recovery of valuable materials is now among the most challenging of current urban problems. We hope that this volume contributes some understanding to this complex and perplexing problem.

CHAPTER 2

THE SOLID WASTE
MANAGEMENT PROBLEM

The purposes of this chapter are to overview northern New Jersey's solid waste management problems and to define the limits of this research project. Briefly, the study area's solid waste problems seem to be far more serious than those faced by other metropolitan regions. They emanate from the same sources that afflict other regions: increasing waste generation, decreasing availability of disposal sites, and stricter environmental regulations.

Northern New Jersey has been brought to an early, critical, and unavoidable decision point because of the waste generated by its massive population concentrated in a relatively small area amid the largest megalopolitan region in the world. On the one hand, the huge amount of solid waste generated in the region will soon overwhelm conventional solid waste disposal practices. On the other hand, the severity of the problem offers a fertile and perhaps unparalleled ground for testing the efficacy of new solid waste technologies at their most efficient scales.

Northern New Jersey's solid waste management problems and limits of the research study will be presented in four stages: (1) urban America's solid waste management problems; (2) the New York region's solid waste management problems; (3) northern New Jersey's acute solid waste management problems; and (4) limitations of the research.

URBAN AMERICA'S SOLID WASTE MANAGEMENT PROBLEMS

During the last decade, like so many resource management problems, solid waste disposal has become a serious problem for urban regions. In most urban areas the days of

the inexpensive haul of solid waste from the curb and backyard to a nearby dump are over. The quickly out-of-sight,
out-of-mind approach to solid waste disposal can no longer
be conveniently practiced in the face of too much waste,
too many environmental restrictions, and too few disposal
sites.

Since the United States became an urban nation about
1920, the volume of solid waste has substantially increased.
In urban regions, some of this increase may be attributed
to the nation's population increase and to the urbaniza-
tion of the population. Between 1920 and 1970 the urban
population of the United States increased from about 55
million to almost 150 million.

Another factor has been the affluence of the society,
which has encouraged the marketing of throwaway products.
The amount of waste generated on a daily per-capita basis
has risen from 2.75 pounds in 1920 to about 5.3 in 1968.

The demand for higher standards of living has led to
more solid waste and has fundamentally changed the nature
of the solid waste stream. Many new products and packages
have been created which are not readily degradable or
economical to reuse. As these products are discarded, their
different character makes them potential public health
hazards.

More than 90 percent of the waste material has been
deposited on the land where rain and natural leaching has
moved contaminants into surface water and groundwater.
Some of the trash has been burned, contributing to air pollution. Open dumps have been a breeding ground for rat
populations and other disease vectors. Both open dumps
and sanitary landfills are eyesores in urban regions, which
find themselves increasingly unable to hide their disposal
sites. Finally, landfills have become considerably more
expensive to operate because of increasing land costs and
environmental regulations designed to minimize the environmental
degradation of the landfill.

During the 1930s, incineration became a popular alternative to landfilling and dealt with 5 to 10 percent of the
solid waste. Forty years later, most of the approximately
300 large refractory incinerators have been closed down
because they are hopelessly in violation of air quality
standards.

Finally marginal, vacant land, readily accessible to
urban centers for low-cost disposal, has become a scarce
commodity. When urban communities find potential sites,
they are usually faced by a set of seemingly insurmountable
problems beyond the normal processes of collection, processing, and disposal. The sites may be to close to residential
developments, which engenders high land costs and an irate

citizen reaction, especially if the waste is to come from
another political jurisdiction. Alternatively, the proposed
site may be near water courses and therefore face opposition
from environmental interests and water supply managers. Or
it may be near one of the urban airports, in which case the
site may be dismissed a priori because of a fear of plane
crashes caused by bird populations. The rare site that engenders little opposition may be unacceptable for the
following reasons: the terrain is unsuitable; the site is
inaccessible to the hundred or more heavy trucks that would
haul to a 200-to 300-acre site; and it is too remote from
a source of clean fill used to cover the waste.

Summarizing, the genesis of the urban solid waste problem follows the by now standard path which has turned the
provision of public services like water supply, transportation
and education from relatively uncomplicated and inexpensive
duties which could be handled on an ad hoc basis to complex,
expensive tasks which require many years of preplanning.

The increasing difficulty of managing solid waste led
the federal government to pass legislation aimed at assisting
local government through financial and technical assistance,
research, and demonstration projects.[1] Prior to the 1965
federal act, only two states had solid waste management programs and few states had disposal regulations which reflected new environmental standards. Ten years later more than
half the states had solid waste laws, rules, and regulations,
including permits, governing disposal, and provisions for
technical and financial assistance.[2]

The 1965 and 1970 federal acts for the most part, however, left implementation in the hands of state, county,
and local governments. The Council of State Governments
has argued that strong state action will be necessary because most local governments are unable to meet the federal
mandate of the solid waste acts and the environmental requirements of the federal and state water and air quality
acts.[3]

While the federal and state governments may provide
the direction toward resource recovery and regionalization
and some of the financial and technical assistance, the
burden for implementation has largely fallen to local
governments, which have three basic choices:
    (1) continue landfilling by increasing the landfill
        area, through alteration of the material by compact-
        ion, or by raising the heights of the fills;
    (2) reduce the amount of potential waste through legis-
        lation designed to discourage throwaways; and
    (3) move toward resource recovery or long-haul.

Landfilling was and is likely to be the choice for most urban regions that have available sites and therefore do not have to take a gamble on the new recovery technologies. For example, Stanley Consultants recommended a combination of landfilling and transfer stations to Cuyahoga County, Ohio, an area of about 4,500 square miles containing more than 2 million citizens. Landfilling was recommended to the communities (including Cleveland) because it is relatively inexpensive in that area and because it is a technology which is proven and adaptable to newer technologies.[4] Similar recommendations were made by the consulting firm Camp, Dresser and McKee to Erie and Niagara counties, New York.[5] As in the Cuyahoga case, the two counties (containing about 1.3 million residents) can continue to landfill if the local communities (including Buffalo and Niagara Falls) cooperate. Finally, Day and Zimmerman prepared what might be labeled a standard recommendation for a smaller urban region.[6] Their advice to Mercer County, New Jersey, with a population of about 300,000, was to continue sanitary landfilling and to move toward compaction as landfilling space becomes tight.

In conclusion, while the county solid waste plans we have examined recognize the problems of increasing waste generation and increasing expense, and the need for regional management, they by-and-large advocate landfilling wherever it is economically feasible because it is a proven method of disposal.

Waste reduction may be achieved through such mechanisms as container laws, tax and deposit requirements, and recycling programs Oregon and Vermont have passed mandatory deposit laws. Many other states have studied recycling and the legislation of both states. Relatively few have passed legislation.[7] Frankly, as yet, unlike the World War II period, large-scale recycling does not seem to have gained much acceptance.

Finally, research into resource recovery technologies has produced a variety of technologies that are being funded as demonstration projects. Baltimore has constructed and has begun limited operations on a 1,000-ton-per-day gas pyrolysis plant. The recovered gas will be sold, as will recovered ferrous metal and glass. St. Louis has been operating a facility which converts solid waste into a dry fuel that is a substitute for coal. These two well-known and othe projects may be emulated elsewhere as the pressure on landfill sites increases and as the price of fossil fuels rises. Overall, however, the expansion of landfill areas, the use of transfer stations, and the compaction of waste to save space appear to be the options most regions have selected for solid waste management through the mid-1980s.

THE NEW YORK REGION'S SOLID
WASTE MANAGEMENT PROBLEMS

In 1973,the Council of State Governments concluded
that "solid waste disposal problems have become acute in
the larger urban centers of the United States. The problem is most acute in the large metropolitan belts, called
megalopolises."[8] Two years earlier the Tri-State Regional
Planning Commission had nominated the New York region to
the dubious distinction of the region most seriously affected by solid waste problems.

> We in the Tri-State Region have the most cri-
> tical solid waste problems in the nation, sim-
> ply because we don't have the vacant land on
> which to throw waste away. Of the three major
> types of pollution besetting urban areas, solid
> waste is the one in which we continue to lose
> ground.[9]

A brief consideration of some of the New York region's
problems should suffice to demonstrate the serious nature
of the problem.[10] First, three-fourths of New York City's
25,000 tons per day of solid waste have been disposed of
by landfilling and one-fourth has been disposed of by incineration. New York faces a serious disposal gap by 1980.
The 5,000 to 10,000 tons per day of waste brought to the
New Jersey meadowlands from New York have been blocked by
the Hackensack Meadowlands Development Commission (HMDC).
It seems unlikely that ocean dumping, banned in 1933, will
be allowed again. New York has looked at conventional
and unconventional incineration, at resource recovery, and
even at the possibility of constructing a mountain after
the West Berlin example to turn the waste problem into an
asset.[11]

Westchester and Nassau counties, New York, lie respectively north and east of New York City. While they do not
face the staggering problem of disposing of 25,000 tons
of waste each day, they have faced disruption of their normal practices. Much of Westchester County has relied on a
landfill at Croton Point. In mid-1972 the federal government sued Westchester County to preserve streams and tidal
marshes of Croton Point. This suit marked the first inter-
vention by the government to protect marshland along with
requesting the court to order separation of reusable
materials.[12] Facing this suit, Westchester has moved cau-
tiously toward resource recovery.

Nassau County has relied on incineration for half of
its solid waste disposal. While many people prefer incineration to landfilling, Nassau's incineration program
has been disrupted by air quality violations. For example,

in North Hempstead, a landfill site which was to last for
a decade was filled in four years because the local incinerator was closed due to air quality regulations.[13]   The problem is countywide.   In June 1975, five municipal incinerators in Nassau County were cited for violations of state
and federal clean air standards.[14]

     To the west of New York City, northern New Jersey faces
the closing of the Hackensack Meadowlands landfill sites, a
problem which will be considered in detail in the next section.

     In conclusion, a survey of the New York region's solid
waste management system confirms our interpretation of the
national literature.   As environmental regulations are en-
forced, closing unsatisfactory landfills and incinerators,
resource recovery systems will become increasingly attract-
ive.   They are likely to be developed in densely settled
regions which do not have an inexpensive landfilling option
and which have a large mass of solid waste generated in a
relatively concentrated geographical region.

NORTHERN NEW JERSEY'S ACUTE
SOLID WASTE MANAGEMENT PROBLEMS

     Northern New Jersey has been spoiled by the availability
of centrally located marshlands.   Long before the 1965
federal solid waste management legislation, northern New
Jersey had a regional solid waste solution: landfilling
the marshes, fields, and streams of the Hackensack Meadowlands.   The decision of the Hackensack Meadowlands Development Commission (HMDC), a body authorized by the state of
New Jersey to manage the Meadowlands, to end inexpensive
landfilling has prompted the resource management crisis examined in this study.

An Overview of the Regional Setting
of the Hackensack Meadowlands

     The Hackensack Meadowlands is a unique island of open
land amid the densely developed counties of northern New
Jersey.[15]   The approximately 20,000 acres of the Meadowlands are composed of organic silt and marshes which are
subject to both fresh-water and salt-water flooding.   These
physical characteristics have retarded development of the
area.   While the Meadowlands have not been suitable for normal residential and commercial development, they have been
seen as emminently suitable for noxious activities legally
banned or otherwise unsuitable for other portions of the
New York region.   Accordingly, most of the approximately
7,500 committed acres of the Meadowlands are devoted to such
activities as roads, rails and yards, airports, warehouses,

transmission lines, storage tanks, and industry. These activities frequently adjoin landfills, which presently receive
about 45,000 tons of solid waste each week, and open space
and streams which have attracted flocks of fowl and fish
both rare and widely distributed in the United States.

The Role of the Hackensack
Meadowlands Development Commission

The piecemeal and haphazard development of the Meadowlands led to the creation of the HMDC in 1968. With respect
to solid waste management, the critical powers of the HMDC
are to approve and to direct land use in the district. As
part of its master plan for the Meadowlands district, the
HMDC plans to phase out five of the six remaining inexpensive
landfills by the spring of 1977 and the last by 1979. In
addition, in order to aid in the construction of its 2,000-
acre recreation area the HMDC plans to shred, compact, and
bale solid waste as building blocks. The charge for baling
is estimated at $7 per ton compared to the current Meadow-
lands disposal charge of $2.50 to $4 per ton. In the words
of William McDowell, executive director of the HMDC:

> People from outside the Meadowlands have been
> dumping here cheaply for years. And now its
> only fair that they help pay the costs of turn-
> ing it from dumps to parks.[16]

The people from outside the region include more than
100 northern New Jersey communities and communities from
New York State. In the 1940s the combination of the economic legacy of a depression and the material needs of World
War II constrained the amount of waste to be landfilled.
However, with the conclusion of the war and the beginning
of suburbanization and growing affluence, the Meadowlands
became a centralized, regional dumping ground. By 1968
it was receiving 29,000 tons per week. Five years later,
Meadowlands landfills were receiving 55,000 tons per week
of solid waste.

The huge increase in landfilling threatened to wipe
out the planned Meadowlands parkland before the master
plan could even be adopted. Accordingly, in 1971 the HMDC
began to make policy decisions which have inexorably led to
northern New Jersey's acute solid waste management problem.
In 1971 the HMDC adopted sanitary landfill regulations and forbade filling virgin wetlands.[17] In 1972 the HMDC closed down a landfill which was receiving New York waste and banned liquid
waste disposal.

In 1973 garbage from outside New Jersey was banned. This policy, which reduced the input by 10,000 tons per week, has been legally challenged, but remains in effect at the time of this writing. Overall, between 1970 and 1975, the number of acres of available landfill space in the Meadowlands has decreased from 2,500 to about 650.

While it was curtailing landfilling, the HMDC was seeking a substitute for landfilling because it is legally obligated to provide a means of disposal to 118 northern New Jersey communities which have been using the Meadow-lands. Two early attempts (1970-72) were a 6,000-ton-per-day incinerator and a 400- acre site in a rural New Jersey county, 50 miles west of the Meadowlands.[18] More recently, the HMDC has been studying the baling option and a set of resource recovery proposals.[19]

The Solid Waste Management Crisis in the Meadowlands Service Area

The Meadowlands service area has a legal definition and a functional definition. The legal definition is the obligation of the Meadowlands to provide a means of disposal for 118 northern New Jersey communities that had been disposing some waste in the Meadowlands. The function-al definition which we have adopted for use in this study differs from the legal definition in three respects. First, we have included 136 communities in the study area, whereas the Meadowlands are obligated to serve only 118. The 136 communities represent all the minor civil divisions in the approximately 500 square miles of the following northern New Jersey counties: Bergen, Essex, Hudson, Union, and southern Passaic (Exhibit 2.1). Legally, 112 of these 136 communities are permitted to use the Meadowlands. The re-maining 24 are located in communities which were using other disposal sites, some of which have now been closed, at the time of the survey that established the Meadowlands legal region. It is our view that these 24 communities would seek to use any inexpensive recovery alternative or land-fills constructed in the Meadowlands because of their lo-cation near the Meadowlands and a lack of other alternatives.

On the other hand, we have eliminated 6 of the 118 legally allowable communities from the functional region. These 6 lie in Middlesex and Monmouth counties and are more likely to use landfills and recovery sites currently under study or operating in their counties. Summarizing, the waste source region for our Meadowlands region consists of 136 communities located in five northern New Jersey counties:

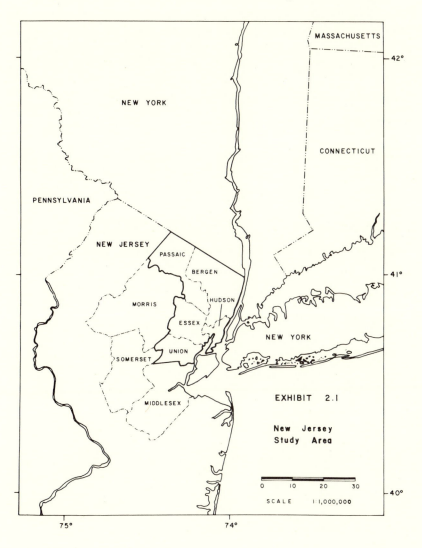

MASSACHUSETTS

42°

NEW YORK

CONNECTICUT

PENNSYLVANIA

NEW JERSEY

PASSAIC

BERGEN

41°

MORRIS

HUDSON

ESSEX

NEW YORK

UNION

SOMERSET

EXHIBIT 2.1

MIDDLESEX

New Jersey
Study Area

0   10   20   30

SCALE   1:1,000,000

40°

75°   74°

112 are already legally entitled to use the Meadowlands and 24 others are likely to use Meadowlands facilities in the near future.

The third difference between our functional definition of the Meadowlands region and the legal obligations of the HMDC is that we have included some disposal sites in the following three counties which are adjacent to the five waste source counties in our functional region: Morris, Somerset, and Middlesex. This decision is a reflection of the fact that these disposal sites are sufficiently close to the waste source counties to be disposal options.

While the HMDC has been eliminating the region's ideal, centralized, and inexpensive landfill solution, a combination of environmental regulations, the increase of waste generation, and the spread of development eroded most of the other inexpensive landfilling and incineration options available to the Meadowlands service area.[20] In 1968 the Meadowlands region sent more than half of its waste to the Meadowlands.[21] Landfills available to the region as of late 1974 are listed in Exhibit 2.2. The 38 special-use municipal disposal areas include compost areas and sites limited to bulky items, leaves and trees which were not composted, and demolition wastes. The 16 special-use private disposal areas include those limited to demolition wastes, trees, brush, and the disposal of septic tank wastes. The 12 other facilities include sites used by institutions, other public agencies and those used for on-site industrial disposal.

For management purposes only the 51 conventional landfill sites can be counted on for the disposal of the region's solid wastes. The life expectancy of these 51 conventional landfill sites are categorized by location in Exhibit 2.3. On the surface, our projection of the life expectancy may seem unusually pessimistic. However, it agrees with recent regional trends. Specifically, between 1971 and 1973, 26 landfills in the study area were closed; only three new landfills were opened.[22] Five of the six incinerators were closed. Furthermore, several of the Meadowlands landfills were closed while we were making the study. Only four of the 13 landfills lie within the waste generation source region, a fact which implies great political vulnerability on the part of the five waste source counties to the adjacent counties.

Within the Meadowlands service region Bergen County faces the most acute problem.[23] Much of Bergen is located far from the disposal sites in the adjacent areas of the region, even assuming the construction of transfer stations, and is running out of county disposal sites. In early 1975

EXHIBIT 2.2

SOLID WASTE DISPOSAL AREAS
1974 TABULAR SUMMARY BY OWNERSHIP AND FACILITY TYPE

County	--- MUNICIPAL --- Conventional Landfill	Special Use Landfill	-----PRIVATE----------- Conventional Landfill	Special Use Landfill	Other Landfill Facilities	Total
Bergen	2	19	5[a]	2	1	29
Essex	1	6	-	3	2	12
Hudson	1	-	4	1	-	6
Passaic	1	-	2	1	-	4
Union	2	2	-	-	-	4
Total Source Area	7	27	11	7	3	55
Morris	5	6	5	5	1	22
Middlesex	7	5	8	3	6	29
Somerset	8	-	-	1	2	11
Total Adjacent Areas	20	11	13	9	9	62
Total Region	27	38	24	16	12	117

[a]Includes one county landfill open to the general public.

Source: Tabulations of the New Jersey Department of Environmental Protection.

EXHIBIT 2.3

SOLID WASTE DISPOSAL AREAS, 1974 and 1980:
CONVENTIONAL LANDFILLS

Location	1974	1980[a]
Hackensack Meadowlands	10	1
Remaining Source Region	8	3
Adjacent Areas	33	9
Total Region	51	13

[a]Source: Analysis of capacities of the facilities and
plans for the facilities and amounts of waste
received at sites.

a number of community sites were closed because of groundwater pollution. These communities began to haul to the
more distant Bergen County landfill sites. However, two
weeks after their new hauls began, one of the Bergen County
landfills was closed. This landfill site had been serving
26 towns (about 325,000 people) for 15 years. Bergen
County was denied permission to landfill into virgin marshlands. Instead, one of the existing Meadowlands landfills
was opened to these communities. Summarizing, within a
two-month period some drivers of sanitation vehicles in
Bergen County must have thought that they were learning a
maze, rather than disposing of solid waste.

Overall, the Hackensack Meadowlands service region
faces an immediate and a long-range solid waste disposal
problem. By mid-1977 more than 100 communities with over
3.5 million residents will not have any inexpensive disposal alternatives. Unless a relatively inexpensive resource recovery system is on line within the near future,
the residents of the Meadowlands face a series of unpala-
table choices: the opening up of new landfills in their
communities; the destruction of the remaining open-space
sanctuaries in the Meadowlands at a high environmental and
economic cost; long-hauls out of the region to nearby regions by truck or to distant regions by rail.

LIMITATIONS OF THE RESEARCH

The serious solid waste management problems faced by
the Hackensack Meadowlands service area are the focus of
this research project. Our concern is with four components
of the waste management system: waste generation, transportation, processing, and disposal. The study does not
deal with the storage and the collection of waste. These
two components typically account for between half and four-
fifths of the waste disposal cost to a community. They include such considerations as the following: type of storage container; location of pickup (backyard, curb, or other);
method of financing the system; and frequency of pickup.
These variables may significantly affect total system cost.
They are not, however, important considerations influencing
the choice of the ultimate disposal technologies and sites.

Accommodations were made to time, cost, and information
limitations. First, the 136 communities in the study area
were collapsed into 25 refuse sheds (Exhibit 2.4). This
step reduced the number of calculations of travel costs,
population, and waste generation by a factor of five. In
addition, we estimate that the computer costs were reduced
by at least a factor of five.

EXHIBIT 2.4

SPATIAL DISTRIBUTION OF WASTE SHEDS

	Number of Communities	*Number of Waste Sheds*
Bergen	70	8
Essex	21	5
Hudson	12	2
Passaic	12	5
Union	21	5
Total	136	25

Four rules were followed in preparing the aggregations. County boundaries were preserved in recognition of the strong possibility that the county may assume an important management role. All waste sheds were grouped from contiguous communities. The minor civil divisions were grouped along major transportation paths and/or were planning units within the counties for which special data tabulations were available. The projected solid waste loads were located at the population centroid of each of the waste sheds.

The loss of information about individual communities is more than made up by the fact that we were able to test many more technology/location/transportation/price alternatives than we would have been able to test with a system of 136 waste sheds. Furthermore, reasonable estimates can be made for each community by disaggregating the waste shed results to the communities.

A second accommodation to the realities of financial and information constraints was made in selecting landfill sites for the model. In choosing existing landfills, our objective was to include large sites which might be functioning by 1980. Using these two criteria, the number of existing landfill sites was reduced from 51 to six. The reduction was achieved in two steps. First, all landfills with capacities of less than 450 tons per week which are located in the source region were accommodated by subtracting their waste capacity from the waste generated in the waste shed in which they are located. For example, suppose a waste shed has a landfill which has been receiving 200 tons per week. For the 1975 run, we subtracted 200 tons per week from that waste shed's waste generation. In reality, few of the small landfill sites are expected to be open by 1980. Therefore, their impact on the model runs is negligible.

A more important step was the aggregation of disposal site capacities in the two multiple landfill areas: the Hackensack Meadowlands and Middlesex County. The six remaining Meadowlands sites were merged into one site in Kearny and the four Middlesex County sites located along the Raritan River in Edison and East Brunswick were aggregated to a single Edison site. This step was taken for three reasons. First, it greatly reduces the number of waste-source-to-ultimate-disposal paths. Second, it recognizes the fact that no one seems to know precisely which landfills are used by which carters. Had we had unlimited research staff and computer time, we would have connected each waste shed to each existing landfill. We did not, however, have these resources. Moreover, travel-time measurements indicated that the sites were located so close to one another that the cost estimates for only the adjacent waste sheds might be biased by the aggregations.

The selection of future landfill sites is literally as well as figuratively a hazardous assignment. None of the state and county officials was willing to share with us possible sites or even site-selection criteria. Since this dearth of information had been expected, we devised three criteria for choosing representative sites. One guideline was that wherever possible each county should be assigned at least one major landfill site. The second and third criteria were that regional landfills require at least 200 acres of vacant land and excellent road accessibility. Through a process of elimination, we learned that representative sites could be found in communities which have at least 200 acres zoned for industrial use and access to one or more interstate or county roads. When a county had many communities meeting the industrially zoned land and accessibility criteria, in order to minimize the transportation costs we tested several alternatives but found that the model chose the community closest to the mass of the Hackensack service region's population. Further review of the selection process is found in Chapter 7.

Finally, the scope of the study was limited to seeking alternative solutions to the region's solid waste management problems through 1985. We did not investigate the indirect economic and environmental impacts of the technology/site/scale combinations. We did not conduct field and library investigations of the new sites chosen for landfills or resource recovery systems, nor did we determine if the resource recovery systems would overtax the transportation, water, and other resources and services of their regions. Such investigations are planned for the near future.

NOTES

1. The two federal acts are the Solid Waste Disposal Act of 1965 (PL 89-272; October 20, 1965) and the Resources Recovery Act of 1970 (PL-91-512, October 26, 1970). For summaries of federal activities and responsibilities, see the annual reports of the Council of Environmental Quality.

2. Environmental Quality: The Third Annual Report of the Council on Environmental Quality (Washington, D.C.: G.P.O., 1972), pp.173-175.

3. The Council of State Governments, The States Roles in Solid Waste Management (Lexington, Ky: Council of State Governments, 1973), p.ix.

4. Stanley Consultants, Inc., Cuyahoga County Solid Waste Management Plan: 1972-1995 (Cleveland, Ohio: Board of County Commissioners, 1973).

5. Camp, Dresser and McKee, Erie and Niagara Counties Comprehensive Solid Waste Study, vol. 1, for the New York State Department of Environmental Conservation and Erie and Niagara Counties Regional Planning Board (Boston: Camp, Dresser and McKee, 1972).

6. Day and Zimmerman, Inc., Solid Waste Disposal Study and Plan: Comprehensive Planning Program, for the Mercer County Improvement Authority (Philadelphia: Day and Zimmerman, 1971).

7. For a general review, see Environmental Quality: The Fourth Annual Report of the Council on Environmental Quality (Washington, D.C.: G.P.O., 1973), p.204. For more specific evaluations, see the testimony of Oregon Environmental Council Regarding S. 2062 before the Senate Commerce Committee in Washington, D.C., May 6, 1974 (8 pages). For an example of one county that has adopted legislation, see Beverage Container Deposit Legislation Study Committee, Social, Economic, and Environmental Impacts of the Beverage Container (Auburn, N.Y.: Cayuga County Environmental Management Council, 1973).

8. The Council of State Governments, 1973 report, op.cit., p.9.

9. Solid Waste Problems, Proposals and Progress in the Tri-State Region (New York: Tri-State Regional Planning Commission, 1971), p.1.

10. A good overview is presented in the source cited in
     note 9.

11. A number of articles about New York City's problems
     have appeared in the New York Times. The most thorough
     is "Problems of Ridding City of Garbage Eludes a Solu-
     tion," New York Times, March 24, 1970, p.49.

12. "Government Sues Westchester over Pollution at Croton
     Point," New York Times, May 10, 1972, p.28.

13. See Solid Waste Monitoring (New York: Tri-State Re-
     gional Planning Commission, 1974), p.3, and Tri-State
     Regional Planning Commission, 1971 report, op.cit.,
     p.3.

14. U.S. Environmental Protection Agency, Region II, Region
     II Report, New York City (June 1975), p.1.

15. See Hackensack Meadowlands Development Commission,
     News Release, Lyndhurst,N.J., May 14, 1975, and
     "Hackensack Meadowlands," official zoning map, adopted
     November 18, 1972 for general descriptions of the HMDC,
     the area, and the development plan.

16. Remarks made to our group on May 28, 1975, at offices
     of HMDC, Lyndhurst, N.J.

17. The chronology of policy decisions was published by the
     HMDC in mimeographed form in May 1975.

18. The HMDC's review of the 400-acre site in rural Warren
     County, N.J., is discussed in the New York Times,
     November 27, 1972, p.39.

19. A faculty group from Farleigh Dickinson and Stevens
     Institute of Technology made preliminary evaluations
     of eight resource recovery options that had been sub-
     mitted to the HMDC (An Analysis of Solid Waste Processing
     Proposals for the Hackensack Meadowlands Development
     Commission, Teaneck, New Jersey, 1973). The firm of
     Burns and Roe is now evaluating the baling-shredding
     system and doing exploratory work on a dry fuel system
     (conversation with William H. Wechter, supervising
     environmental engineer, May 28, 1975, Lyndhurst, N.J.).

20. See New Jersey Department of Environmental Protection,
     Rules of the Bureau of Solid Waste Management, NJAC,
     7:26-1 et seq., July 1, 1974, for a review of the en-
     vironmental regulations.

21. Based on tabulation secured from the HMDC and the New
     Jersey Department of Environmental Protection.

22. Tri-State Regional Planning Commission, 1974 report, pp. 23-24.

23. Bergen County's problems have been frequently described in the <u>Bergen Record</u> in April and May 1975.

CHAPTER 3

THE MATHEMATICAL MODELS

In this chapter, we review three different mathematical models that have been used in this study of solid waste management. The three algorithms that will be discussed include: (1) an equation set devised by the authors for use within standard linear programming applications; (2) a fixed-charge model developed for the federal Environmental Protection Agency (EPA) by Roy F. Weston, Inc. and Argonne National Laboratories; and (3) a new version of the EPA model that is currently being developed by Mitre Corporation.[1] All three models are similar insofar as they have an objective function representing the sum of the disposal costs, the haul costs, minus revenues, which is to be minimized subject to a set of constraints including waste quantities and facility capacities.

A cursory glance at the three models suggests that the fixed-charge models developed for EPA [(2) and (3)] would clearly be preferable to the linear model because the EPA models are capable of directly evaluating facility economies of scale in a single run. In contrast, the linear model treats economies of scale by repetitive test runs of different scale plants. There are, however, other considerations which favor the linear model. In the course of this chapter we will review the equations, structures and the requirements of the three models with respect to data requirements, ease of program modification, computer costs, and manpower.

THE RUTGERS MODEL

The first algorithm to be considered was developed by the authors for use on solid waste problems. The model

itself has been implemented on an IBM 370/158 utilizing the
system resident linear programming package Mathematical
Programming System (MPS) as developed by IBM. This "canned"
program allows a user to tailor the MPS language to conform
to any linear programming algorithm. In this particular
situation, four basic constraints plus an objective function
are used. Before each is discussed in detail, a brief review
of the basic notation follows. In this model, the following
subscripts are used: (1) i denotes a source of waste; (2) j
refers to an intermediate facility for waste processing, specifically a resource recovery plant; (3) k denotes an ultimate
site, specifically a landfill or power plant; and (4) T refers to a transportation link over which the waste travels.

Objective Function

The purpose of the systems model is to minimize the region's total costs. In order to accomplish this, the objective function and its associated constraints are designed to
account for a real-world situation, yet seek out the combination of least system cost. The linear objective function in
this model is as follows:

$$\text{Minimize } Z = \Sigma_i \Sigma_j C_{ij} T_{ij} + \Sigma_i \Sigma_k C_{ik} T_{ik} +$$

$$\Sigma_j \Sigma_k C_{jk} T_{jk} \tag{1}$$

where C = the cost in dollars per ton associated with all
possible travel links in the system.

In the linear model the link cost includes the travel cost,
and the charge at the facility (capital and operating) minus
any revenue from sale of the waste products.

Constraints

1. Source Balance

$$\Sigma_j T_{ij} + \Sigma_k T_{ik} = S_i \quad \text{(for } i = 1 \ldots m\text{)} \tag{2}$$

where S_i = the amount of waste generated at each source
of solid waste input.

m = the number of sources in the system.

This equation represents the movement of waste away from the source nodes. In each case, all waste must leave the origin and be conveyed over the transportation links to either intermediate facilities (j) or final sites (k). There can be no storage or waste residue at a source, as the quantity of waste generated must equal the sum of the waste transported over the sytem links.

2. Intermediate Facility Capacity

In this case, we must assure that each intermediate facility in the system cannot accept more waste than its physical capacity allows. Therefore:

$$\Sigma_i T_{ij} \leq K_j \ \ (for \ j = 1 \ldots n) \tag{3}$$

where

    K_j = the capacity in tons per week for each intermediate facility in the system.

    n = the number of intermediate facilities.

The same constraint is also true for ultimate sites.

3. Ultimate Facility Capacity

$$\Sigma_i T_{ik} + \Sigma_j T_{jk} \leq K_k \ \ (for \ k = 1 \ldots \mu) \tag{4}$$

where

    K_k = the capacity in tons per week for each ultimate facility in the system.

    μ = the number of ultimate sites.

Here, waste can arrive directly from a source (i) or as residue from an intermediate process (j). The total acceptable quantity cannot exceed the capacity (K) of the ultimate site.

4. Intermediate Facility Balance

The final equation has been used successfully alone or as part of a dual constraint that permits direction of the waste residue or recovered materials. The general form of the equation is:

$$\Sigma_i PT_{ij} - \Sigma_k T_{jk} = 0 \ \ (for \ j = 1 \ldots n) \tag{5}$$

where

P = the percent of waste remaining at site j after intermediate processing has been completed. This amount may be usable recovered material, residue or both.

n = the number of intermediate facilities.

This equation states that whatever quantity of waste exists at an intermediate facility after processing must be disposed of at an ultimate facility or be removed from the system. For example, a P of .6 indicates that 60 percent of the original waste stream remains to be dealt with and that 40 percent of that initial amount has been removed from the system. The recovered material may include such products as glass, paper, and ferrous metal. Consumers of these products can be included in the system as final sites. For example, gas pyrolysis techniques can convert 80 percent of a waste stream into a usable gas product; the other 20 percent is extracted and sold to external industries. In such a case, P would equal .8, since it is the remaining gas product that must now be dealt with in the system. In some cases, two or more balance constraints are used in tandem to trace the destination of the products. For example, consider:

$$\Sigma_i PT_{ij} - \Sigma_k T_{jk} = 0 \ (for \ j = 1 \ldots n) \qquad (5a)$$

$$\Sigma_i \beta \ T_{ij} - \Sigma_k T_{jk} = 0 \ (for \ j = 1 \ldots n) \qquad (5b)$$

where

P = that percent of the waste remaining at the intermediate facility that must be disposed of in one unique manner (for example, dry fuel).

β = that percent of the waste remaining at the intermediate facility that must be disposed of in another unique manner (for example, landfilling).

n = the number of intermediate facilities in the system.

Here P is .60 for the dry fuel and β is .15 for the landfill system. If only one balance equation was possible, the difference between the dry fuel product and the residue product would be indistinguishable and, therefore, an inaccurate model of reality. As we shall see with the subsequent models, such flexibilty is grossly lacking in the nonlinear algorithm, which leads to some severe problems that will be touched on later.

The total of 75 percent denotes the fact that a dry
fuel plant installed as an intermediate facility extracts
25 percent of the initial waste stream for use outside the
system, for example, in steel mills or glass factories.
The proportion taken out of the system in this study is
related to the availability of information about the specific locations of markets for recycled materials and to
our conservative approach as to the availability of markets
for recycled products.

Inputs, Time, and Costs

Basic data on waste quantities, facility capacity, and
travel times are standard for each of the models. The
linear model requires that the transportation links include charges for the capital and operating costs of the
sink node, the transportation cost, and revenue savings.
New cost coefficient calculations must be undertaken for
each potential link at a different operating size and
facility cost level. For example, one set of link costs
are computed under the assumption that the waste will be
taken to 2,000-ton-per-day plants. A second link coefficient set assumes that the waste will go to 1,000-ton-
per-day plants. If a run indicates that a specific facility is unlikely to receive its waste capacity, then its
associated cost links are changed to reflect the lower
capacity facility. Hand manipulation of the program deck
is time consuming, and the multiplicity of cost calculations can be tedious. Therefore, for the Rutgers model,
factors such as data requirements, program handling, and
manpower needs must all be regarded as moderate to high.
In short this iterative process is not elegant; however,
it works.

In terms of computer costs, each run costs no more
than $2.60 based on educational rates of $.08 per comput-
ing second for a system consisting of 319 transportation
links. The method is extremely cost effective. From the
machine perspective perhaps the most important point is
its intermediate facility balance flexibility. As already
mentioned, the other models could not simulate the multiple
destinations of the waste as well as the linear model.
This advantage makes it hard to beat in its ability to
approximate real-world solid waste options so closely.

THE EPA MODEL

At this point, we are no longer dealing with a standard linear programming model. The work completed for EPA

by Roy F. Weston Associates and subsequently by Argonne
National Laboratories, utilized a fixed charge, nonlinear
programming algorithm developed by Warren Walker. The
justification for this approach is that for the case of a
solid waste problem, while the system constraints are
linear, the initial fixed cost of the system's facilities
involve economies of scale and therefore nonlinear cost
functions. The previously discussed linear model accounts
for these economies by multiple program runs in arriving
at an optimal solution. The fixed-charge models are able
to reflect these concave cost functions within the same
program execution through the use of the Walker algorithm.
The algorithm approximates these nonlinear functions by
using piecewise linear segments or with logarithmic, semi-
logarithmic, or linear functions. In this way, thresholds
for the entire function are established with each linear
segment representing a further increase in the economy of
scale for each particular site. To account for these
piecewise functions the subscript notation in the following models reflects this segmented scheme. In the Rutgers
model, i referred to a source, j to an intermediate facility, and k to an ultimate site. Since the algorithm itself
will determine the economies involving the j and k terms,
each subscript now denotes a "site/process/linear segment"
to be associated with a waste transfer. The advantage of
such a procedure is that the algorithm is able to assign
the most suitable process at the most economical linear
segment to each particular intermediate and final site
in the system. The original implementation by Weston
utilized a $\Sigma_m F_m Y_m$ term added to the objective function
to account for the fixed costs (F) of each facility (m),
while the Y element represented a dummy variable that
brought a facility cost into the function only if that
facility was utilized. Therefore, the intermediate and
final facility capacity constraints that we have seen
earlier were expanded to accept a second segment:

$$\Sigma_i (T_{ij} + T_{ij'}) \le K_j \; (for \; j = 1...n) \qquad (6)$$

where
$\quad$ j' = the larger intermediate facility segment.

And for the ultimate sites

$$\Sigma_i (T_{ik} + T_{ik'}) + \Sigma_j (T_{jk} +$$
$$T_{jk'}) \le K_k \; (for \; k = 1...\mu) \qquad (7)$$

where
$\quad$ k' = the larger final facility segment.

The Weston model was developed to handle a maximum of two segments in the nonlinear cost curve; a limitation that does not constrict the Argonne or Mitre efforts. The following equations refer to the Argonne version of the EPA model.

Objective Function

The objective function of the equation set is devised to minimize total system cost over the transportation links that comprise the system. Here, however, the added fixed-charge dimension is accounted for separately from the transportation cost:

$$\text{Minimize } Z = \Sigma_i \Sigma_j C_{ij} T_{ij} + \Sigma_i \Sigma_k C_{ik} T_{ik} + \Sigma_j \Sigma_k C_{jk} T_{jk} +$$

$$\Sigma_j C_j P_j + \Sigma_k C_k P_k \tag{8}$$

where

C = the cost associated with all possible travel links in the system or the costs of the intermediate and final facilities.

P_j or P_k = the amount of waste processed at the intermediate or ultimate site.

Constraints

1. Source Balance

As before, all waste must be removed from each source to either an intermediate or a final facility. In this case, the j and k subscripts reflect the site/process/segment assigned and not merely a site.

$$\Sigma_j T_{ij} + \Sigma_k T_{ik} = S_i \quad (for \ i = 1 \ldots m) \tag{9}$$

where

S_i = the amount of waste generated at each source of solid waste input.

m = the number of sources in the system.

2. Intermediate Facility Processing

$$\Sigma_i T_{ij} \leq K_j \quad (for \ j = 1 \ldots n) \tag{10}$$

itself has been implemented on an IBM 370/158 utilizing the system resident linear programming package Mathematical Programming System (MPS) as developed by IBM. This "canned" program allows a user to tailor the MPS language to conform to any linear programming algorithm. In this particular situation, four basic constraints plus an objective function are used. Before each is discussed in detail, a brief review of the basic notation follows. In this model, the following subscripts are used: (1) i denotes a source of waste; (2) j refers to an intermediate facility for waste processing, specifically a resource recovery plant; (3) k denotes an ultimate site, specifically a landfill or power plant; and (4) T refers to a transportation link over which the waste travels.

Objective Function

The purpose of the systems model is to minimize the region's total costs. In order to accomplish this, the objective function and its associated constraints are designed to account for a real-world situation, yet seek out the combination of least system cost. The linear objective function in this model is as follows:

$$\text{Minimize } Z = \Sigma_i \Sigma_j C_{ij} T_{ij} + \Sigma_i \Sigma_k C_{ik} T_{ik} + \Sigma_j \Sigma_k C_{jk} T_{jk} \tag{1}$$

where C = the cost in dollars per ton associated with all possible travel links in the system.

In the linear model the link cost includes the travel cost, and the charge at the facility (capital and operating) minus any revenue from sale of the waste products.

Constraints

1. Source Balance

$$\Sigma_j T_{ij} + \Sigma_k T_{ik} = S_i \text{ (for } i = 1 \ldots m) \tag{2}$$

where S_i = the amount of waste generated at each source of solid waste input.

m = the number of sources in the system.

where

K_j = the capacity in tons per week for each intermediate facility/process/segment.

n = the number of intermediate facilities.

3. Ultimate Facility Processing

$$\Sigma_i T_{ik} + \Sigma_i T_{jk} \leq K_k \ (for \ k = 1...\mu) \qquad (11)$$

where

K_k = the capacity in tons per week for each ultimate facility/process/segment.

μ = the number of ultimate facilities in the system.

Similar to equations (2) and (3) of the Rutgers model, these two constraints prevent a facility from exceeding its physical capacity for the determined process/segment.

4. Intermediate Facility Input Balance

$$\Sigma_i T_{ij} - P_j = 0 \qquad (12)$$

where

P_j = the amount of waste processed at intermediate site/process/segment j.

5. Ultimate Facility Input Balance

$$\Sigma_i T_{ik} + \Sigma_j T_{jk} - P_k = 0 \qquad (13)$$

where

P_k = the amount of waste processed at ultimate site/process/segment k.

These last two equations are the result of changes to the Weston model. Instead of the previously mentioned $F_m Y_m$ term in the objective function, Argonne substitutes the P_m term that defines the amount of waste processed. Its associated C coefficient represents the charge for this processing. However, in order to accomplish this expansion to a greater than dual-segmented solution for both intermediate and ultimate sites and to bring this multisegmenting into the objective function, a different approach to the function was needed.

Weston associates the fixed charge with the following:

$$\Sigma_i T_{im} + \Sigma_j T_{jm} - Y_m = 0 \qquad (14)$$

where

Y_m = the dummy variable needed to credit a positive cost to a facility *(m)* if that facility is used in the solution. It is obvious that this equation established a positive Y for utilized facilities and remains zero for those that are not.

Argonne divides the balance equation into input balance for both intermediate and final sites, with the P term accounting for the objective function input. In this manner, each type of facility is included in the objective function at its own level/segment.

6. Intermediate Facility Output Balance

This equation is similar to (5) of the Rutgers Model.

$$\Sigma_i \beta_j T_{ij} - \Sigma_k T_{jk} = 0 \; (for \; j = 1..n) \qquad (15)$$

where

β_j = the transfer coefficient for intermediate site/process/segment j (or the percentage of waste remaining after processing).

n = the number of intermediate site/processing/ segments.

As before, this equation removes the remaining waste/residue/product from the intermediate facility. However, there is no flexibility, as with the Rutgers model, for providing for more than one type of residue. We feel very strongly that this is a serious drawback to the model, as it cannot accurately reflect state-of-the-art processes. This entire question will be discussed at the end of this section in a review of the mathematical models.

Inputs, Time, and Cost

In relation to the linear Rutgers model, the fixed-charge model requires less input data in the objective function. Since the algorithm is geared to select appropriate economies of scale, the numerous objective function

calculations required by the linear model are replaced
by segmented equations or nonlinear equations. The other
inputs required by the linear and nonlinear models are the
same waste generation figures, facility capacities, and
waste transfer coefficients. The nonlinear model requires
the linear or nonlinear curve type be provided, the P and
β regression equation coefficients associated with the
cost curve, and a threshold at which the equation switch
is desired.

In terms of actual execution, the EPA model has proven
to be expensive to run. A test deck, provided by EPA stop-
ped after using ten minutes of CPU time on an IBM 370/158
without completing the test problem that EPA provided and
at a cost of over $100. As far as our particular applica-
tion is concerned, we have yet successfully to execute
the program on our actual problem deck because of program
malfunctions. A trivial problem (five sources, two inter-
mediates, and three finals) has been run at a cost of
$8.55 per the rates already mentioned. Our most recent
attempt to run the EPA model yielded an amazing result:
the program violated a landfill capacity constraint. Upon
communicating this fact to Argonne, we were told that the
model is not fully debugged or completely documented, a
fact we can definitely attest to! Indeed, we found that
the program will violate a constraint if a linear function
is used in the final optimization stage. The suggestion
to use a log model instead of a linear model to measure
the economies of scale was rejected. Fitting of the real
world to the model is not an appropriate procedure. Overall, due to the constraint violation problem, we do not
have cost figures with which to compare the linear and
nonlinear models.

To the potential user of the Weston/Argonne/EPA model,
we point out the following five additional weaknesses of
the model. First, if you choose to input separate travel
times and turn-around times, you will be rewarded with a
systematic error. We found that when the algorithm doubles
the travel time and adds it to the turn-around time it
subtracts one minute. With this model a 30-minute one-way
travel time and a 20-minute turn-around time equals a 79-
minute trip instead of an 80-minute trip.

Alternatively the user can choose to insert the direct-
haul costs in dollars per ton. Unfortunately, if one of
the options includes a travel cost of greater than $10 per
ton, the user will have to round off the cost because the
input field can take only four digits, of which one is a
decimal. For example, a travel cost of $10.23 per ton
must be rounded off to $10.2 or $10.3.

Third, the user will find that the theoretical elegance of using an equation to measure the operating costs at different plant sizes is diminished. The problem is that the model does not have a separate point to register the revenues accrued from selling the waste products. In the linear model, one subtracts the revenue from the capital, operating, and transportation costs for each link. This cannot be done in the fixed-charge model because the capital and travel costs are inputed separately in forms which are not amenable to a revenue deduction per ton. The revenue, therefore, has to be accounted for in the operating cost equations. The user's equations become net operating cost as a function of size of facility instead of gross operating cost as a function of facility size.

Fourth, while the fixed-charge model reduces the number of runs that need to be made, it increases the number of links which have to be developed in two important cases. In one case, the user may find that one facility receives less than its optimal waste capacity. The linear model will identify the amount by which the plant falls short of its capacity. The analyst can either modify the size of the facility and operating charges on the next run or, in a region like New York, can assume that the difference will be made up by exogenous solid waste inputs from the industrial waste stream or from the biggest waste source in existence: New York City.

The fixed-charge model is not so flexible. If a plant falls short of its capacity, the algorithm penalizes the total system. In order to overcome the penalty, the user must artificially add a new source of waste with a specific link or links.

In the second case, the fixed-charge model forces the user to add links to include the development of a waste recovery facility composed of modular units. For example, assume that one site was proposed to include three 2,000-ton-per-day dry fuel plants. The linear model would input the costs for facility operation on the basis of the cost of a single 2,000 ton-per-day facility. The links could, however, all be directed to the single 6,000-ton-per-day facility.

The fixed-charge model is not easily adapted to a charge at one level and the acceptance of waste at another level. The user can develop two segmented equations, one of which reflects the economics of scale for a single facility, and the second of which is a constant continuing the cost of the single facility. Alternatively, the user has to link each source to each of the modular units.

In either case, the linear model more easily handles the modular facility case.

Fifth, the Weston/Argonne/EPA model does not allow for lower limit constraints and for indivisibilities in solid waste facilities. We doubt that a region large enough to use this model will care to invest in a resource recovery facility of 80 pounds per day. The model should have lower- as well as upper-capacity constraints. In addition, we doubt that plants will be constructed at odd sizes. A manufacturer may be able to scale a facility to the nearest 250 pounds per day but not to the nearest 50, 25, and 10 pounds per day. A linear model can be adapted to integer constraints. The fixed-charge models have not been adapted to indivisibilities.

THE MITRE MODEL

The basic difference between the fixed-charge EPA and Mitre models is that the latter further divides the j and k subscripts into a jpl or kpl notation so that j and k refer to the sites themselves, p to the process at the site, and l to the linear segment governing the economy of the process. As developed by Edward B. Berman, this model purports to account directly for land or site congestion constraints. In the EPA model, each additional linear segment, as a piecewise linear approximation of the concave cost function, is treated, in effect, as a new facility. The Mitre model is designed to solve the same problem as the EPA version but in less computer memory space and therefore at less cost.

Objective Function

This equation is the same as that in the EPA version except for the additional subscripts which represent processes and linear cost segments of processes.

$$\text{Minimize } Z = \Sigma_i \Sigma_j \Sigma_p \Sigma_l C_{ijpl} T_{ijpl} + \Sigma_i \Sigma_k \Sigma_p \Sigma_l C_{ikpl} T_{ikpl} +$$

$$\Sigma_j \Sigma_k \Sigma_p \Sigma_l C_{jkpl} T_{jkpl} + \Sigma_j \Sigma_p \Sigma_l C_{jpl} P_{jpl} +$$

$$\Sigma_k \Sigma_p \Sigma_l C_{kpl} P_{kpl} \tag{16}$$

Constraints

1. Source Balance

As before:

$$\Sigma_j T_{ij} + \Sigma_k T_{ik} = S_i \text{ (for } i = 1...m) \qquad (17)$$

where

S_i = the amount of waste generated at each source of solid waste input.

m = the number of sources in the system.

2. Intermediate and Ultimate Site Processing

For each site there is a constraint:

$$\Sigma_p \Sigma_l a_{jp} P_{jpl} \leq K_j \qquad (18)$$

or

$$\Sigma_p \Sigma_l a_{kp} P_{kpl} \leq K_m$$

where

P_{jpl} = the processing in tons per week at intermediate site j, process p, segment l.

K = an arbitrary large number.

a_{jp} = K/K_{jp} = the "processing coefficient" for intermediate site j, process p.

K_{jp} = the capacity in tons per week of process p at site j assuming that site j were totally devoted to process p. This capacity is related to an available land constraint and a traffic congestion constraint.

3. Intermediate Facility Input Balance

$$\Sigma_i T_{ij} - \Sigma_p \Sigma_l P_{jpl} = 0 \text{ (for } j = 1...n) \qquad (19)$$

where

P_{jpl} = the processing in tons per week at intermediate site j, process p, segment l. The model is free to choose which process and segment to use based on cost minimization.

n = the number of intermediate sites.

4. Ultimate Facility Input Balance

And likewise

$$\Sigma_i T_{ik} + \Sigma_j \Sigma_p T_{jpk} - \Sigma_p \Sigma_l P_{kpl} = 0$$

$$(for\ k = 1 \ldots \mu) \tag{20}$$

for the ultimate sites, except that the input may come directly from the sources or through the intermediate facilities. These equations establish waste quantity figures *(P)* for input into the objective function as described earlier.

Finally:

5. Intermediate Facility Output Balance

$$\Sigma_k T_{jpk} - \beta_p \Sigma_l P_{jpl} = 0 \tag{21}$$

where
β = the transfer coefficient (the fraction of ton output to input) for process *P*.

This is similar to the Argonne version except that here we see a percentage of the processed waste *(jpl)* in the equation instead of the input waste (T_{ij}).

Inputs, Time, and Cost

Since we have not seen the final version of the Mitre model, there are no specifications on it. Mitre does claim it is faster and more efficient than the EPA model. We sincerely hope that its performance will be superior to the EPA model.

SUMMARY

The three basic mathematical models that have been discussed all represent a great deal of time, work and expense on the part of the authors to reflect accurately real-world solid waste processing functions. In comparing these models we have considered all the major characteristics of the models in their static forms and subsequently have weighed one against the other.

Required Input

All the models demand waste generation data, transportation linkages, facility capacities, and transfer coefficients as mandatory inputs. The linear path of the
Rutgers model requires the user to calculate the actual
link costs for different economies of scale. The nonlinear
models require capital costs, operating cost equations, a
starting haul cost, and travel and turn-around times so that
the algorithm can calculate the minimum costs in the objective function.

In essence, the inputs to the different models are the
same. The more elegant models, however, perform the analyses with fewer runs. Frankly, we feel that the submission
of decks to the computer is trivial, since the same data
must be collected and it is the data collection which con-
sumes the vast majority of the time.

Manpower, Time, and Costs

We cannot exactly compare the models, since the two
fixed-charge models have not produced useful results. The
linear model requires a moderate-to-high amount of manpower
to implement, since the linear nature of the model demands
that the user prepare all the required cost calculations and
undertake a series of trial runs before arriving at an
optimal solution. Some may consider this unwieldy, others
not. We found the additional work and runs to be more re-
warding in information than costly in time. We cannot,
however, be the judge of this criterion for another user.

Our limited and frustrating contact with the Argonne
model leads us to think that, if its numerous programming
difficulties can be corrected, the deck manipulation and
manpower will prove to be minimal for its execution. We
cannot comment on the Mitre version since we have not been
able to use it because of a missing front-end (input) pro-
cessor.

As far as computer costs are concerned, the Rutgers
model is the most cost effective. However, a working version of the Argonne and, subsequently, Mitre models may
prove to be economical to use.

Simulation of New Technologies

This last and most important criterion does not, at
the present time, speak well for the fixed-charge EPA models.

The basic flaw of these algorithms lies in the intermediate facility balance equations. Weston and Argonne in their attempts to provide for a piecewise linear approximation of a nonlinear cost curve ignored the present state-of-the-art technology in their handling of waste transfer coefficients. Their models allow for the removal of a percentage of the waste from the system, while the remainder must be dealt with in only a single transfer. This option is satisfactory for an incinerator or transfer station where the resulting product is either ash or compressed waste. Newer technologies such as dry fuel, and gas and oil pyrolytic systems, produce several different types of waste products and recovered products. The EPA models are unable to cope with these technologies other than by artificially converting an intermediate facility into a source which cannot help but lead to an estimation error.

Summarizing, at the present time we would not recommend the use of the Weston/Argonne/EPA models because of basic flaws in the programming. In the long run, assuming that the fixed-charge model programming is improved, one faces the tradeoff between the added computer costs and complexity of the fixed-charge model versus the additional keypunching and deck setups and submissions of the linear model. Given the inherent limitations of the transportation and waste generation data and the fact that indivisibilities will undoubtedly become the rule in the construction of solid waste systems, we have concluded that there is no advantage to be realized from using the fixed-charge model in regions which have a limited number of sources and facility options. Frankly, the model overpowers the input data. In regions which have 25 or more sources of waste and a dozen or more options of dealing with the waste, we recommend that the basic choices be calculated with the linear model and that the fixed-charge model, where operational, be used to fine-tune the results and to make sure that the most desirable of the two or three best solutions has been identified.

NOTES

1. The following documents have been useful in understand-
    ing the fixed-charge model: W. Walker, A Heuristic
    Adjacent Extreme Point Algorithm for the Fixed Charge
    Problem (New York: Rand Institute, June 1973); Roy F.
    Weston, Inc., Development of a Solid Waste Allocation
    Model, West Chester, Pa.: Roy F. Weston, Environmental
    Scientists and Engineers, July 1973); E. B. Berman,
    A Model for Selecting, Sizing, and Locating Regional
    Solid Waste Processing and Disposal Facilities (Bedford,
    Mass.: MITRE Corporation, October 1973); and H. J.
    Yaffe, Note on Equation Structures and Sizings of the
    EPA and MITRE Solid Waste Allocation Models (Bedford,
    Mass.: MITRE Corporation, May 1974).

CHAPTER 4

SOLID WASTE GENERATION

This chapter reviews the waste-generation projections made for the years 1975, 1980, and 1985. The model required the development of population projections and waste-generation rates for the 25 source areas in the five-county region. The chapter is divided into three parts: (1) population estimates; (2) per-capita waste estimates; and (3) estimated solid waste generation in the study area in 1975, 1980 and 1985.

PROJECTING THE REGION'S POPULATION

Two approaches were available for producing the projections: (1) use existing projections, or (2) prepare a systematic set for the entire study area. After evaluating the methodologies and assumptions of the existing projection sets, it was decided to develop estimates.

Summary of Existing Population Projections

Five sets of projections were available. Bruce Newling developed a set of projections from a minor civil division (MCD) base for all the 136 minor civil divisions in the study area.[1] His modified exponential model assumes that every community will move toward either an urban, suburban, or rural density by increasing or decreasing in population density. Newling's model places local growth in the context of intraregional trends in suburbanization. Taken alone, however, the model lacks the capability to consider changing birth and death rates directly.

The Port Authority of New York and New Jersey prepared projections for the New York metropolitan region to
the year 1990. While the methods are not described in detail, previous publications prepared by the agency indicate
that U.S. census projections are used as a starting point
and are distributed to the region based on the recent historical record.[2]

The New Jersey Bell Telephone Company approached the
problem of projecting the state, county, and MCD populations in three steps.[3] The first step projects total population as three components of population change: births,
deaths, and net migration. For any given year, the population is estimated to be the previous year's population, plus
births, plus net migration, less deaths. The Bell component
estimates show an accelerating increase in population through
1985.

In the late 1980s Bell projects that population growth
will begin to slow down as the birth rate declines and net
migration falls. This slowing trend will continue through
the year 2000.

The second step is the Hagood-Siegel method for small-
area population projection. Population is distributed
throughout the state on a county basis and then redistributed
throughout the county on an MCD basis. This is done by
apportioning population to each area based on the historical
record of each population unit.

The third step takes into account local circumstances
which may affect population. Additional information was included, depending upon the availability of data for each
municipality. These included updated census information and
Bell staff knowledge of area potential for growth. Several
assumptions were also made in an attempt to fine-tune the
projections, including the following: the decline and re-
vitalization of cities; the shifting of population growth
from the northern and eastern sections of New Jersey to the
southern and western regions; urban to suburban shifts in
population being replaced by suburban to rural shifts; and
New Jersey continuing to attract retired persons to senior-
citizen and retirement villages in the south and central
parts of the state.

No mention was made as to the credibility of these
assumptions, nor were empirical data supplied to substantiate these assumptions. Overall, the report shows increasing populations for all five counties at relatively constant
rates.

The New Jersey Office of Business Economics discussed in general terms their basic approach to estimating the current state population.[4] The estimations for each MCD were based on the final data supplied by the 1970 census. Detailed information including new migration factors, size of family, vacancy rates, housing turnover, measures of natural increase, and numbers of building permits issued were taken into account for these estimates. Using 1973 estimates as a base, population projections were made on the county level for the years 1975 through 2000 by five-year intervals. Unfortunately, the office was unable to provide any insight as to the nature of their projection methodology. Upon observation, it appears that the state figures were increasing at fairly constant growth rates and increments through 1985.

Estimates prepared for the counties were a fifth source of projections. In October 1973 the Essex County Department of Planning, Economic Development and Conservation published its most recent population projections up to the year 1990 in five-year intervals.[5] Methodology was not discussed, nor was information obtainable from the department. A review of their figures shows growing increments in population for each five-year interval.

The only current population projections for Bergen County were those obtained from a 1970 water study by Elam and Popoff, engineers.[6] The methodology was not described in the text of this study and additional information as to its adequacy was not made available. Since the projections were made for the years 1975,1980, 1990, and 2000, logarithmic interpolation between the years 1980 and 1990 was used to obtain 1985 figures.

The Hudson County Planning Board published its most recent population projections in 1970 for five-year intervals up to the year 2000.[7] No information was provided as to how these figures were derived. It can be seen from the results that moderately stable increases were predicted for the county overall.

The Passaic County Planning Board report, *Passaic County Municipal Population Projections to Year 2000* had, by and large, the most complete explanation of the methods used to obtain estimates.[8] A few of the inputs that were considered include zoning and subdivision regulations, housing market trends, master plan studies, projected transportation improvements, and various other municipal improvements. Each minor civil division was analyzed individually, considering special population factors that were applicable to the situation. A discussion of these growth factors was included in the text for all the MCDs in the county.

In their solid waste disposal management program, the Union County Planning Board had separately contracted Hammer, Siler and George Associates to prepare population projections for the county.[9] The overall plan for Union County appeared to be a sophisticated study, but it was rather odd that the county expects to decrease in population from now until the year 2000. Neither a methodology nor any assumptions were given to explain this decrease.

Comparison of Existing Projections

The five existing sources of population projections summed over the five counties are compared in Exhibit 4.1.

EXHIBIT 4.1

Variation of Existing Projections
Over Five-County Study Area

	1975	1980	1985
Newling	3,469,055	3,577,897	3,695,934
Bell	3,541,920	3,647,280	3,779,240
State	3,580,820	3,727,520	3,881,260
Port Authority	3,470,000	3,522,000	3,614,000
County	3,557,052	3,684,200	3,786,504

The difference between the highest projections (state of New Jersey) and lowest (Port Authority) is 267,000 in 1985, or about 7 percent. As one moves from the total regional scale down to the county scale and to the 25 solid-waste-shed areas the differences between the projections become magnified. By 1985 several of the waste-shed variations were as high as 40 percent.

Final Estimates

Having compiled the population projections of the five-county study area, it became apparent that the county projections varied so much in assumptions and methods that they could not be used as absolute numbers. However, it would be

an error to disregard completely the counties' own projections, since they reflect local knowledge and are sensitive
to economic and social trends in their communities.

In an effort to preserve the advantages inherent in
using projections prepared at the county scale, and at the
same time in order to maintain a uniformity which would
lend credibility to our population projections, a step-down
method approach developed by the author and others was
utilized.[10] The method uses a chain of alternative techniques which allows variables or models most appropriate for
each geographic scale to play their role in the projection.
For example, cohort-survival techniques are inappropriate
for a township, but appropriate for the nation. Land-hold-
ing-capacity techniques are inappropriate for the nation,
but appropriate for the township. Each technique has its
level of greatest competence and the chain model permits
each to play its role with a minimum of distortion to the
others.

The approach is illustrated by Exhibit 4.2. It begins
by adopting a set of cohort projections for the nation to
the target year and then extends state-level cohort survival
projections to the target year, controlling these extensions
with the national total. Next, the model analyzes the distributional properties of county projections and adjusts
them to the state totals previously developed. Alternatively, the user may choose to insert national or county projections into the model, thereby shortcircuiting the chain. The
advantage of shortcircuiting the chain is that the user may
wish to test the implications of alternative projections prepared at the state and county levels with economic base or
development policy underpinnings. The model finally moves
to the minor civil division (MCD) level.

At the MCD level three types of options are available.
One simply extrapolates the past 50 years of record, com-
putes a vector of proportions, and multiplies the resulting
proportions by the county constraint. A second option in-
troduces county planning board or regional agency projections, analyzes the distributional properties of these estimates, and adjusts them to the county constraints. A
third option, using a density ceiling model to prepare MCD
projections, converts these projections into a matrix of proportions, and adjusts them to the county constraints.
Finally, the model includes an allocation routine for dis-
tributing the MCD projections to regions delineated by the
user.

EXHIBIT 4.2

A FLOW DIAGRAM OF THE GREENBERG/KRUECKEBERG/MAUTNER
MODEL FOR LONG-RANGE POPULATION PROJECTIONS

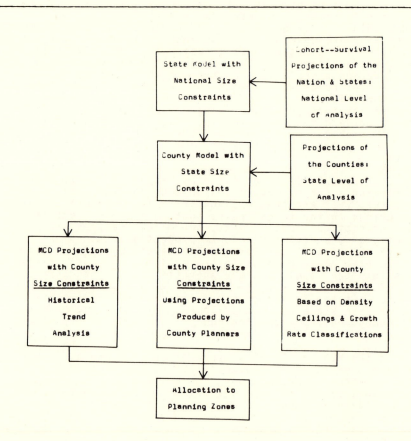

For this study the path indicated in Exhibit 4.3 was used. Specifically, we chose to use the most recent population projections made by the state of New Jersey for the counties and by the counties for the MCDs. The step-down procedure was repeated for all 136 MCDs in the study region, except in the case of Bergen County where the large number of municipalities made the waste-shed subregion aggregates a more convenient working unit.

The final estimates are listed in Exhibit 4.4. The reader should note that the total for the 25 waste sheds is always slightly less than the state total shown in Exhibit 4.1 because northern Passaic County was not included in the study area.

SOLID WASTE GENERATION

This section develops current and future estimates of daily per-capita waste-generation rates for each of the 25 subregions in the study area. These rates can then be multiplied by the estimated population of each region to arrive at an estimate of total waste production.

For the purposes of this analysis, solid waste was defined as being comprised of the following: (1) household waste, which includes putrescible waste, rubbish, and non putrescible waste normally generated by individuals or families; (2) household bulky waste referring to large items such as stoves and refrigerators disposed of by households; (3) yard debris including lawn clippings, tree trimmings, and the like coming from ordinary yard maintenance; (4) street sweepings, which refers to the waste collected from maintenance of public roads such as dirt and catch-basin cleanings; and (5) small commercial waste coming from small retail stores, restaurants, and the like that may be located on regular collection routes of regular household waste haulers. For convenience and clarity, the foregoing categories will be designated as municipal solid waste.

Solid wastes produced by large commercial establishments and industrial facilities were excluded due to the specialized nature of these wastes, which are normally collected and disposed of by private, contracted haulers.

Estimating Present Waste Generation

The first task was to estimate current municipal waste-generation rates. Data were available in computer printout

EXHIBIT 4.3

A FLOW DIAGRAM OF THE PROCEDURE USED
TO ESTIMATE THE POPULATION

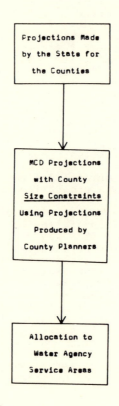

EXHIBIT 4.4

POPULATION PROJECTIONS
FOR TWENTY-FIVE WASTE SHEDS,
1975 -85

	Waste Shed	*1975*	*1980*	*1985*
Bergen	1	58,732	65,545	72,998
	2	73,142	81,579	91,148
	3	30,415	35,539	40,448
	4	88,675	95,739	104,284
	5	326,533	344,134	363,963
	6	115,579	.119,837	126,204
	7	134,245	142,548	151,188
	8	122,429	130,339	138,917
Hudson	9	235,132	244,433	253,973
	10	379,157	371,657	364,427
Passaic	11	54,615	60,060	65,933
	12	40,863	42,919	44,635
	13	149,137	153,124	157,223
	14	37,870	40,701	43,844
	15	143,640	149,442	155,797
Essex	16	42,875	53,105	65,987
	17	219,739	227,898	234,613
	18	57,914	64,756	71,110
	19	256,720	259,330	259,789
	20	373,963	365,970	354,030
Union	21	53,888	57,229	60,431
	22	120,486	126,818	133,617
	23	119,605	126,360	132,346
	24	181,331	191,600	203,107
	25	100,959	106,445	112,708
Total		3,517,644	3,657,117	3,802,720

from the Bureau of Solid Waste Management of the New Jersey State Department of Environmental Protection.[11] This information included the total amount of solid waste collected by each hauler from every municipality in the state.

The information was reported as total solid waste, and there was no breakdown as to what proportion constituted municipal waste. An attempt was made to factor out all haulers that appeared to service major industries or businesses. All haulers collecting less than 2,500 cubic yards per year were excluded because they would be delivering waste to the disposal site no more than three times per week. Since municipal waste requires a more intensive effort, an assumption was made that these haulers were either specific industrial/commercial waste haulers or small operators hauling negligible amounts of waste.

Next, the amounts of waste collected by haulers that were identified as serving only industrial or commercial customers were subtracted from the total municipal waste figure. It was assumed that municipal waste would be the largest figure left for each town. Dividing this by the population of each region produced the per-capita generation rate.

The results of this approach (Exhibit 4.5) are extremely erratic. Generation rates were produced ranging from less than 2 pounds per capita per day to greater than 50 pounds per capita per day! A few municipalities, such as Mahwah, were reported as producing no solid waste at all, while other municipalities were not even listed.

Conversations with officials in the bureau also gave the impression that much of the information was not accurate because most collectors keep rather poor records of the actual weight of the waste that they haul. Thus, amounts reported to the bureau are mainly the product of guesswork done to satisfy legal requirements rather than being a product of accurate accounting. In addition, it was believed that under-reporting might be practiced to avoid providing regular information that could be used in tax investigations. Further analysis of this data-set was considered to be fruitless due to its dubious quality.

Another attempt to estimate generation rates was made with a model which assumed relationships between per-capita generation and residential density, income, type of housing, family size, and age of the population. Several examples of the density approach exist in the literature: the Roy F. Weston Solid Waste Study for Macon County, and the Cuyahoga

EXHIBIT 4.5

PER-CAPITA WASTE-GENERATION
ESTIMATES DEVELOPED FROM NEW
JERSEY STATE DEPARTMENT OF
ENVIRONMENTAL PROTECTION DATA

	Waste Shed	Gross from State Data	Municipal Waste After Analysis
Bergen	1	5.8	5.2
	2	1.8	1.5
	3	3.7	3.5
	4	3.4	3.3
	5	2.4	1.4
	6	3.1	2.6
	7	9.3	6.2
	8	4.2	3.1
Hudson	9	4.7	1.9
	10	6.0	2.4
Passaic	11	7.1	4.5
	12	5.4	4.5
	13	9.2	6.7
	14	8.3	6.5
	15	5.6	2.5
Essex	16	57.7	55.1
	17	11.4	10.5
	18	4.1	1.6
	19	7.7	6.7
	20	7.2	3.1
Union	21	11.6	6.6
	22	5.5	3.4
	23	6.1	3.2
	24	5.6	2.6
	25	6.7	3.5

County Solid Waste Management Study. According to the latter study, such a relationship would exist for two reasons.[12]

    (1) Densely populated areas are likely to be served by
        a more efficient collection system thus encourag-
        ing higher disposal rate.

    (2) Sparsely populated areas offer more opportunity
        for on site storage or for illegally disposing
        of waste materials in isolated or vacant areas,
        fields, or open ditches.

Empirical proof was not offered to substantiate either of
these assumptions and, frankly, while the second assumption
could probably be sustained by survey, the first assumption
seems unreasonable. Nevertheless in order to test the
hypothesis, a scattergram was made of the log of density as
a function of waste generation for the MCDs in Union and
Essex counties. The Union County study from 1973 and the
Essex County study from 1970 provide individual rates for
each municipality.[13] The scattergram did not exhibit a
systematic pattern.

      Other data also imply that at least in our study area
there is no systematic relationship between density and per-
capita solid waste generation. For example, Trenton, New
Jersey, has a relatively high population density and a high
per-capita generation rate; Princeton, New Jersey, has a low
density, but an even higher generation rate.[14] Finally, the
authors of the Erie-Niagara comprehensive solid waste study
argue that density plays no role in waste generation except
for street sweepings and commercial waste. The amount of
litter and commercial activity concentration will increase
along with density.[15]

      Next, an attempt was made to relate municipal waste
generation to the level of income in a community. This test
assumes that as income rises, purchases will rise and thus
the amount of waste will increase. Again, however, no relationship was found. A poor city like Trenton had a higher
generation rate than Princeton Borough. However, wealthy
Princeton Township had a higher rate than Trenton. Similarly, in 1970 Newark, a poor city, had a generation rate of a
full pound per day higher than that of Essex Fells, one of
the wealthiest towns in the United States. The Louisville
Metropolitan Regional Solid Waste Disposal study reported
that while higher-income groups produce more paper waste,
lower-income groups produce more metal and glass waste.
Therefore, there was little variation in the waste-generation rates by income.[16]

Next, attempts were made to test the relationship between per-capita waste generation and type of housing unit
or family size. Hale reported that single-family homes in
low-income areas produced more residential waste than
multifamily homes in low-income areas.[17] We tested and rejected the hypothesis that the proportion of single-family
units was related to residential per-capita solid waste
generation. Finally, we tested and rejected the hypothesis
that smaller families and an older population generate less
residential solid waste.

Summarizing, contrary to our expectations based on
water-demand literature,[18] we could not find any variables
which were systematically related to per-capita solid waste
generation. The negative research finding may have three
causes. First, there indeed may not be any systematic relationship between the variables we chose and waste generation. Second, other variables such as price of waste removal, local packaging, and frequency of removal may be the
causative agents. Third, the dependent variable measurements of per-capita residential solid waste may be
inaccurate.

Data were obtained for Hudson County from Tom Greiner,
executive director of the Jersey City Incinerator Authority.[19]
The data were based on thorough and consistent weighing of
all trucks both before and after dumping at the incinerator.
By this method, a municipal generation rate of 2.2 pounds
per capita per day was observed. This was the lowest of all
the regional per-capita rates. According to Greiner of the
Jersey City Incinerator Authority, the higher rates in other
communities came about because most other officials count
trucks, assuming they are filled to capacity, rather than
actually weighing them. Frequently the trucks are partially filled, over-estimating the total weights. Greiner's
observation was supported by data received from Ewing Township, New Jersey, which also weighs the waste before incineration and reports a per-capita estimate of about 2
pounds per person.[20]

Overall, while we were and remain very skeptical about
the base-period waste-generation estimates, we had no choice
but to use the best available studies. The rates developed
by the Union and Essex Counties studies were used for the
respective regions located in those counties.[21] The methodology for the Essex study was unknown; the Union study did
utilize some of the state data, which were considered to be
at best partially accurate. The lack of other credible
available data left little choice but to use these rates.
The rate for each region was determined by taking the
weighted average of the municipal rate contained in that
region.

EXHIBIT 4.6

PER CAPITA GROWTH RATE ESTIMATES FROM THE LITERATURE

Study	Yearly Increment
1. Hunterdon Co., N.J.	.164
2. Musto Commission, N.J.	.146
3. U.S. Public Health Service	.100
4. Erie-Niagara	.095
5. Essex Co., N.J.	.090
6. Mercer Co., N.J.	.085
7. Union Co., N.J.	.082
8. Cuyahoga Co.	.078
9. Tocks Island, N.J.	.070
10. Tri-State Region, N.J. portion	.070
11. American Public Works Association	.070
12. Lakeland Region B	.045
13. Lakeland Region A	.039
14. Oakland Co.	.035
15. Central New York Plan	.030
16. Weston method, applied to New Jersey	.008
17. New Jersey Solid Waste Management Plan	.000
Median:Total	.070
Median:New Jersey	.082

SOURCES FOR EXHIBIT 4.6

1. Hunterdon County Planning Dept., Soiid Waste Management Study, 1971.

2. County and Municipal Government Study Commission, Solid Waste: A Coordinated Approach, Trenton, N.J., September 1972.

3. A commonly quoted number.

4. Camp, Dresser and McKee, Erie and Niagara Counties Comprehensive Solid Waste Study, Vol. I, Grand Island (New York: Erie and Niagara County Regional Planning Board, July 1972).

5. Planners Associates, Inc., Comprehensive Master Plan: Solid Waste Disposal and Collection Study for Essex County, New Jersey, September 1972.

6. Day and Zimmermann, Inc., Solid Waste Disposal Study And Plan, #20 (Trenton, N.J.: Mercer County Planning Board, July 1971).

7. M. Disko Associates, Solid Waste Disposal Management Phase II (Elizabeth, N.J.: Union County Planning Board, July 1974).

8. Stanley Consultants, Cuyahoga County Solid Waste Management Plan 1972-1995, Board of County Commissioners, Cuyahoga County, Ohio, January 1973.

9. Candueb, Fleissig, and Associates, Tocks Island Regional Interstate Solid Waste Management Study, for the Tocks Island Regional Advisory Council, August 1969.

10. J. Lerner, and R.T. Wood, Solid Waste Problems, Proposals and Progress in the Tri-State Region: A Reconnaissance, (New York: Tri-State Regional Planning Commission, August 1971).

11. A widely quoted rule-of-thumb figure.

12. and 13. Pandullo, Chrisbacker, and Associates, Lakeland Regional Solid Waste Report, Lakeland County Planning Board, May 1973.

14.   Jones and Henry Engs., Ltd., <u>Proposal for a Refuse Disposal System in Oakland County, Michigan</u>, Final Report on a Solid Waste Demonstration Grant Project Washington, D.C.: U.S. Government Printing Office, 1970.

15.   Malcolm Pirnie, Inc., <u>Comprehensive Solid Wastes Management Plan</u>, Vol. I (Syracuse: Central New York Regional Planning and Development Board, October 27, 1971).

16.   R.F. Weston, Inc., <u>Macon County Solid Waste Management System Analysis</u>, Project No. 40.00 for state of Illinois (Chicago: Institute for Environmental Quality, April, 1974).

17.   Planners Associates, INc., <u>New Jersey State Solid Waste Management Plan</u> (Newark, N.J.:   Bureau of Solid Waste Management, Department of Environmental Protection, State of New Jersey, July 31, 1970).

In order to determine rates for the other regions, phone interviews were made with the respective area offi- cials. Due to the lack of any method of determining in- dividual town rates from the information given by county officials, a uniform rate was used for each of the regions in the respective counties. The Bergen County rates were based on data supplied by the Bergen County Public Works Department.[22] They were based on records kept at two county landfill sites. Household waste, which included some small commercial and yard debris, was added to household bulky, yielding a municipal waste-generation rate of 3.28 pounds per capita per day.

The Passaic regional rates were developed from infor- mation provided by officials from Paterson, Wayne, Clifton, and Passaic. The information was based on their assessment of changes since the publication of the Quad City Solid Waste study.[23] It was then aggregated into one rate of 3.0 pounds per capita per day for all areas in the county.

Estimating Per-Capita Waste Generation in 1980

The next task was to develop future municipal waste- generation rates from these base-year rates. In the ab- sence of a valid predictive model, a survey of the litera- ture was made to determine the growth rates used by other studies. Seventeen studies were collected and their incre- mental changes in general rates ranked from high to low (Exhibit 4.6). A median of .07 pounds per capita per day was calculated. To determine the rate for the study region, it was decided to use the median of the studies concerned with New Jersey only. The median was used to minimize the effect of extreme values and to prevent special conditions which may have affected the rate in other areas from having any influence. The final incremental growth rate used in this study was .082 pounds per capita per day. This figure is slightly higher than the .07 rate used by Tri-State and flies in the face of recent reports that the leveling off of the economy has produced a leveling off of solid waste generation; but it is somewhat below the Public Health Service .10 rate and the rate used by the New Jersey Musto Commission.

The .082 rate was used to normalize all the base year rates to 1975 and then to project the rates for 1980 and 1985. A summary of these rates in daily form is shown in Exhibit 4.7. Municipal waste totals were then determined by multiplying the per-capita municipal waste rates by the respective populations (Exhibit 4.8).

EXHIBIT 4.7

ESTIMATED PER-CAPITA WASTE
GENERATION: 25 WASTE SHEDS, 1975-85

	Waste Shed	1975	1980	1985
Bergen County	1	3.36	3.77	4.18
	2	3.36	3.77	4.18
	3	3.36	3.77	4.18
	4	3.36	3.77	4.18
	5	3.36	3.77	4.18
	6	3.36	3.77	4.18
	7	3.36	3.77	4.18
	8	3.36	3.77	4.18
Hudson County	9	2.20	2.61	3.02
	10	2.20	2.61	3.02
Passaic County	11	3.00	3.41	3.82
	12	3.00	3.41	3.82
	13	3.00	3.41	3.82
	14	3.00	3.41	3.82
	15	3.00	3.41	3.82
Essex County	16	5.01	5.42	5.83
	17	5.54	5.95	6.36
	18	5.36	5.77	6.18
	19	6.23	6.64	7.05
	20	6.11	6.52	6.93
Union County	21	4.20	4.61	5.02
	22	4.60	5.01	5.42
	23	4.56	4.97	5.38
	24	4.69	5.10	5.51
	25	4.26	4.67	5.08

EXHIBIT 4.8

ESTIMATED MUNICIPAL WASTE
GENERATION: 25 WASTE SHEDS, 1975-85

	Waste Shed	Tons/Week		
		1975	*1980*	*1985*
Bergen County	1	592	741	915
	2	737	923	1,143
	3	307	402	507
	4	894	1,083	1,308
	5	3,291	3,892	4,564
	6	1,165	1,355	1,583
	7	1,353	1,612	1,896
	8	1,234	1,474	1,742
Hudson County	9	1,552	1,914	2,301
	10	2,002	2,328	2,642
Passaic County	11	573	717	882
	12	429	512	597
	13	1,566	1,828	2,102
	14	398	486	586
	15	1,508	1,784	2,083
Essex County	16	752	1,007	1,346
	17	4,261	4,746	5,222
	18	1,086	1,308	1,538
	19	5,598	6,027	6,410
	20	7,997	8,351	8,587
Union County	21	792	923	1,062
	22	1,942	2,224	2,535
	23	1,911	2,198	2,492
	24	2,979	3,420	3,917
	25	1,507	1,740	2,004
Total		46,426	52,995	59,964

THE PROJECTED RESIDENTIAL WASTE, 1975-85

The results indicate that the region's municipal solid waste will rise 29 percent or 13,000 tons per week between 1975 and 1985. In most public facility development analyses, the size of the projected demand is a critical decision-making parameter. The size of the projected increase may be the determining factor as to whether a sewage treatment plant, a public water supply, a school, or some other facility should be expanded. In this case, the 13,000-ton-per-week increase would require approximately one 2,000-ton-per-day plant or a number of smaller facilities. Whether the region generates 46,000 or 60,000 tons of municipal waste per week should not, however, be the decisive factor in the decision to use landfill or resource recovery methods. The 46,000 tons estimated to be generated in the region in 1975 is sufficient to require a number of new facilities and/or sites in the Meadowlands or elsewhere. The additional 13,000 tons projected for the period 1975-85 would require a modular expansion of the basic decision about what to do with the wastes.

In addition to the magnitude of the solid waste generated in the region, two critical considerations are the composition of the waste and the spatial distribution of the waste sources. The composition of the waste is discussed in chapters 6 and 7. In essence, we have assumed that the composition of the waste in 1980 and 1985 will not be significantly different from the composition of the waste in 1975. We have assumed that in this study area there will not be massive paper recovery or legislation which will drastically reduce the amount of ferrous metal products arriving at the processing facilities.

Finally, with respect to the development of resource recovery facilities, the dense concentration of population in the immediate vicinity of the Meadowlands and the electric generating stations in northern New Jersey strengthen the economic case for resource recovery. In 1975 we estimate that the nine waste sheds within a 10-to 15-minute drive of the Meadowlands (5,7,8,9,10,15,17,19, and 20 see Exhibit 4.8) produced almost 30,000 tons of waste per week. This huge quantity of concentrated waste provides a powerful economic argument for a regional solution involving the economies of scale of large facilities.

NOTES

1. Bruce E. Newling, Population Projections for New Jersey to 2000 by Minor Civil Divisions (New York: City College of N.Y., 1968).

2. Port Authority of New York and New Jersey, People and Jobs: A Forecast of Population, Households, Labor Force and Jobs in the New York-New Jersey-Connecticut Metropolitan Region: 1975-1990 (New York: Port Authority of New York, May 1974); and The Next Twenty Years: 1965-1985 (1966).

3. New Jersey Bell Telephone Company,"Population Projections for New Jersey: 1970-2000," unpublished paper, June 1972.

4. Office of Business Economics, Division of Planning and Research, New Jersey Population Projections (Trenton, N.J.: Department of Labor and Industry, July 1, 1973).

5. Essex County Department of Planning, Economic Development and Conservation, Essex County Population Projections 1940-1990 (Newark, N.J.: Essex County Department of Planning, October 1973).

6. Elam and Popoff, Inc., Bergen County, New Jersey, County Comprehensive Plan Report, Water Facilities (Hackensack, N.J.: Essex County Department of Planning, October 1973).

7. Hudson County Planning Board, Population: Hudson County Estimates 1975-2000 (Jersey City, N.J.: Hudson County Planning Board, 1970).

8. Passaic County Planning Board, Passaic County Municipal Population Projections to Year 2000 (Passaic, N.J.: Passaic County Planning Board, December 1973).

9. Hammer, Siler and George Associates, Populations of Union County's Municipalities (Elizabeth, N.J.: Union County Planning Board, August 1974).

10. Michael Greenberg, Donald Krueckeberg, and Richard Mautner, Long-Range Population Projections for Minor Civil Divisions: Computer Programs and User's Manual (New Brunswick, N.J.: Center for Urban Policy Research, Rutgers University, 1973).

11. Bureau of Solid Waste Management. Data compiled from Registration Statements for a Solid Waste Collection or Hauler, N.J. BSWM-43 (Trenton: Department of Environmental Protection, 1971).

12. Roy F. Weston, Inc., Macon County Solid Waste Management System Analysis, Project No. 40.00 for state of Illinois (Chicago: Illinois Institute for Environmental Quality, April 1974), and Stanley Consultants, Cuyahoga County Solid Waste Management Plan 1972-1995 Cuyahoga County, Ohio: Board of County Commissioners, January 12, 1973), p. 28.

13. Planners Associates, Inc., Comprehensive Master Plan: Solid Waste Disposal and Collection Study for Essex County, New Jersey, September 1972; and M. Disko Associates, Solid Waste Disposal Management Phase II (Elizabeth, N.J.: Union County Planning Board, July 1974).

14. Day and Zimmerman, Inc., Solid Waste Disposal Study and Plan, #20 (Trenton, N.J.: Mercer County Planning Board, July 15, 1971).

15. Camp, Dresser and McKee, Erie and Niagara Counties Comprehensive Solid Waste Study Vol. I (Grant Island, N.Y.: Erie and Niagara County Regional Planning Board, July 1972).

16. Institute of Industrial Research University of Louisville, Louisville Kentucky-Indiana Metropolitan Region Solid Waste Disposal Study, Vol. I. (Washington, D.C.: Bureau of Solid Waste Management, D.C. Public Health Service, HEW, 1970).

17. Samuel Hale, Residential Solid Waste Generated in Low-Income Areas (Springfield, Va.: NTIS, 1972).

18. See, for example, Hittman Associates, Forecasting Municipal Water Requirements, 2 vols. (Columbia, M.: Hittman Associates, 1969).

19. Interview with Tom Greiner, director of Jersey City Incinerator Authority on November 26, 1976.

20. Data received from Carl Yonus indicating weight of material received at the incinerator, November 26, 1974.

21. See note 13, above.

22. Information provided by James Murphy, director, Division of Sanitary Landfills, Bergen County, Department of Public Works, October 14, 1974. Figures obtained from a survey of trucks using the Bergen County landfills.

23. Phone conversation with Mr. Sandor, town engineer of the city of Passaic, December 2, 1975.

CHAPTER 5

TRANSPORTING THE WASTE

The hauling of waste to disposal sites usually is more expensive than paying for disposal. Yet our review of solid waste management studies almost invariably reveals that transportation of the waste has been omitted or has been calculated with data of dubious quality and quantity. The purpose of this chapter is to consider the methods we used to obtain the travel costs between the sources of waste, the intermediate facilities, and the final facilities. The review is divided into three sections: (1) estimation of travel times; (2) selection of the most relevant paths in the system for incorporation into the model; and (3) estimation of transportation costs via direct haul and by transfer stations.

ESTIMATION OF TRAVEL TIMES

Although it is easily determined, distance is generally a poor choice because distance ignores the savings of time possible on high-speed, limited-access roads. Minimization of time is an improvement, yet it may result in an overloading of expressways and ignores the problems of congestion. Cost is the best indicator of traffic assignment. However, the complexity of measuring the individual cost decisions is beyond the capability of most transportation plans.[1]

Literature Review

Until the 1950s, traffic assignment was more of an art than a science. Six methods for obtaining road-travel-time data had been developed:[2] (1) the license plate matching method; (2) spot speed and relate to overall speed; (3) ground or air photographs; (4) interviews of drivers or questionnaires; (5) the arrival-output volume rate method; and (6) the floating car method (moving observer method).

The license plate matching method involves two observers, one standing at each end of the link to be measured. Each records the time and license plate number of vehicles as they pass an observation point. Later the times and numbers are matched up and travel time interpolated from this information. Berry and Sawhill have recommended the number of matchings required to achieve adequate sampling according to the volume and capacity of the roadway.[3]

Spot speed studies, frequently employed by traffic police, use two techniques. The first determines instantaneous speed by using a radar meter which operates on the Doppler principle. As a radio wave is directed at a moving vehicle, its frequency changes in proportion to the target's speed. The second method, like the license plate matching method, employs two observers. Instantaneous speed is approximated by timing an observed vehicle as it navigates a measured course. These methods are convenient, accurate, and easy to operate, but they fail to give volume calculations and measurements of delay time, which affects overall journey time.[4]

Ground or air photographs are similar to spot speed studies and suffer from similar shortcomings. Interviews of drivers or questionnaires tend to be extremely imprecise. The arrival-output method calculates a mean journey time for a traffic stream by timing a test car on successive trips in traffic.[5]

The floating car method has been refined by Great Britain's Road Research Laboratory to the moving observer method. In early transportation studies, this method was considered the standard form of measurement. Three men plus a driver navigate a stretch of road. One observer counts the number of vehicles passing in the opposite direction; a second counts the number of vehicles the test car overtakes and is overtaken by; a third observer times the trip, noting both running and delay time.[6] This process is repeated over the same link, in the same direction, a predetermined number of times. Bruton recommends six, Wells, 12. The results are averaged together and are transformed to average travel time for the link.

With each of the last two methods, it is apparent that the larger the number of test runs, the less likely it is that an aberrant reading will be obtained. If, however, an entire road network has to be studied, some compromise between completeness, cost, time, and reliability must be achieved. Other factors which must be taken into consideration during the survey are time of day, time of week (i.e., weekend or weekday), and time of year. Travel times have been found to vary with all of these factors. Bruton specifies that readings be taken at peak and off-peak hours. When, however, only a few runs are to be made, either peak or off-peak hours should be selected. All test runs must be completed during the same time period so that the structural condition of the path itself is held constant.

Garner and Parsons in their 1973 study compare the license plate matching, arrival-output, and moving observer methods.[7] They conclude that the collection and analysis of data for the first two methods involved similar amounts of work and money, while the license matching method was more than twice as expensive. With respect to the number of test runs required, sensitivity to minute-by-minute variations in the traffic stream, and consistency of results, the arrival-output is superior to all the others.

Interest in the further refinement of the six methods seems to have ceased following major developments during the 1950s. The Chicago Area Transportation Study pioneered the use of a complete geocoding or digitization of transportation network information based on Cartesian coordinates.[8] A geocoding system enables the transportation planner to gather data at a fine unit of geographic detail, such as the street address, to aggregate this information to successively larger units, and to display it with computer mapping and other techniques.

Travel times are the first step in the transportation planning process. The expensive and time-consuming timing of the entire road network by any of the six time-honored methods detailed above was no longer necessary. Initial travel times could be determined by the computer based on link length and posted link speed. A pilot program by the Metropolitan Toronto Planning Board utilized this new process.[9] The basic steps in what is called the capacity restraint method of traffic assignment consist of:

(1) classifying every link in the road network by type, location, and width; (2) determining a volume and speed for
the link based on information gathered in the field; (3)
measuring link length by computer; and (4) determining an
initial travel time by computer by the length and speed of
the link.

This initial value is entered into the program as the
first iteration in determining minimum time paths. Successive iterations can simulate travel and guideway conditions
for any period--past, present, or future.[10]

Work on obtaining empirical travel times seems to have
been reduced because almost any set of convenient travel
times may be used to start the iteration procedure. Recent
studies in traffic assignment seem to lie in the direction
of modifying the initial time-distance formula[11] and in the
development of multiple path assignment techniques.[12]

Sources of Travel Time Data in the Study Area

A number of sources of travel time data were theoretically available. Inquiry produced no evidence that county-
level studies had been carried out. A statewide program
entitled TOPICS has generated a number of travel time studies at the municipal level. These studies for the most part
had generated information in the form of average miles per
hour on road links. In order to convert this information
from running time to journey time it would have been necessary to have determined some measure of delay time. Furthermore, there were far too few of these studies to have
adequately covered our study area.

Only a Morris County speed-and-delay study actually
offered us adequate information. A floating car survey
of major routes in that area included both running and
delay time components of journey time. Each link was driven six times in one direction at peak and off-peak hours.
It was decided to reserve this study as a check on our
later computations.[13]

The Tri-State Regional Planning Commission (TSRPC) for
New York, New Jersey, and Connecticut indicated that they
had a complete set of estimated travel times for our area.
Their study had been carried out by the capacity restraint
computer simulation technique. Initial travel time input
had been a function of whether the roadway allowed turning
movements; was one- or two-way; and the link cost. The
last variable was related to posted speed, signalization,
frequency of accidents, and presence of tolls.[14] Unfortunately, evaluation of these data was not possible because

of the $3,000 cost which Tri-State has placed on the out-
side use of their data.

The New Jersey Department of Transportation offered
their recent travel time study of the entire New Jersey
arterial system. They had utilized the floating car method, which differs from the moving observer method in that
it does not tabulate the number of cars the test car overtakes, is overtaken by, or that pass in the opposite direction. The test-car driver attempts to "float" with the
stream of traffic while one observer times the journey,
thus there is no correction factor for the driver's accu-
racy in gauging the average speed of the flow of traffic.

In the New Jersey case, each link had been driven at
least once and frequently twice. Sometimes, however, the
runs were in opposite directions. While off-peak-hour
trips were the rule, peak-hour trips were often included,
and there were too few runs to justify averaging off-peak-
and peak-hour runs together.

The form of the data, a computer map displaying four-
digit numbers and an accompanying link time printout, implies that a computer simulation capacity restraint study
was the objective of this agency. It quickly became apparent when we began working with the data that, while the
form of a computer simulation study had been followed, the
study itself was grounded in techniques of the 1950s.

The four-digit numbers, which for the most part signi-
fied road intersections (sometimes they represented state,
county, or municipal boundaries, other landmarks, or abrupt
turns in the road), could not be identified as specific
highway intersections. The numbers themselves were chosen
in sequence from 2,000 up, but they had no significance as
to the type of road, volume of traffic, signalization, or
other considerations. Most significantly, the arterial
system was not mapped by the computer.

The absence of this essential feature meant that we
could not identify the intersections of the New Jersey
network and fix them in space. Consequently it was im-
possible for us to locate the sources and sinks of our network on the New Jersey Department of Transportation (NJDOT)
computer map. Furthermore, the map had no identifiable
boundaries, or directional indicators, and the scale of 1
inch to every 8,642 feet was one which no other map of New
Jersey seemed to have. This scale was an accommodation to
the computer plotting device. No map could be found to
overlay the NJDOT map, partly because of the odd scale and

partly because the nodes themselves had been systematically displaced so that the numbers could be read clearly in areas of dense highway development.

DOT personnel explained that their intent was to build predictive equations based on the sampled driving times and on other data gathered from a number of transportation surveys done in the area. In view of this aim, it seems apparent that either of two other methods of travel time calculation would have sufficed. Either they could have calculated "ideal travel" time as in the first iteration of the capacity restraint model or they could have rigorously driven a sample of the network. Creighton suggests that an adequate sample can be obtained by driving 30 to 100 percent of all expressways and 20 to 25 percent of all arterials, if the samples are stratified so that there is a "regular geographic distribution of counts through the area."[15]

Use of the New Jersey DOT Data Set

In order to identify the highways on the computer map, DOT offered us the use of their aerial photographs of the state. These maps, pictures of a 12-mile-square area, had the four-digit numbers hand printed on the highways. In most, but not all, cases these roads were identified by their route number. A·very tedious process of drawing in the entire highway system for the study area from these maps was necessary before the data could be evaluated for use.

Only after the locations of the nodes were abstracted from the aerial photographs to the computer map did other weaknesses of the data begin to emerge. First, some major highways had not been driven. For example, travel times were not available for the three major through routes: the New Jersey Turnpike, the Garden State Parkway, and the Palisades Interstate Parkway. Certain roads had not been completely driven. DOT personnel indicated that when a test drive was felt to be inaccurate, it was omitted from the study. These random links were unaccounted for, thus leaving troublesome gaps in the data set. In tracing the route of a highway in one direction, a link would frequently be found in the opposite direction. For example, in proceeding north on Route 17, a link would suddenly appear that was driven south. Links were driven at all different times of day. Finally, occasional links driven more than once would have such gross disparities in time that it cast doubt on the entire data-set.

At this point, the data were considered so inconsistent that we dropped back to the selective use of the NJDOT data. It was decided to choose the most reliable paths on the computer map and to regress the DOT travel time against airline distances as measured by a ruler on the computer map. Links were chosen on the basis of completeness and consistency of measurement. The paths were stratified by length and location.

Twenty-nine links were measured on the computer map. These measurements were multiplied by the map scale of 1.6 miles to the inch to yield the distance of the path in miles. A link speed was calculated in the following manner. The speed limit was abstracted from the computer printout. The maximum speed for a garbage truck was considered to be 40 miles per hour, to account for the time lost on highways in accelerating and decelerating these large vehicles. In areas where the speed limit was posted at below 40, it was assumed that the truck would travel at the limit.

While selection of these travel speeds was based on observation, a recent study by Olsen and Westley provides a measure of support for these estimates.[16] Their study focused on truck operating times between the metropolitan centers of economic areas as defined by the Bureau of Economic Analysis. An essential input into this measurement process was a determination of truck operating speeds which they assumed to vary given terrain, traffic congestion conditions, and road conditions.

Their results lend credibility to our assumption regarding the maximum speed of a solid waste collection truck on a freeway with a speed limit of 55 miles per hour. The 1970 nonstop truck operating speed for level terrain and a relatively congested level of service on a freeway was computed to be 42.1 miles per hour compared to the 40 miles per hour which we have assumed. On multilane and two-lane highways where lower posted speeds would be anticipated, correspondingly slower speeds of 36.9 mph and 31.9 were reported in the study.

It should be noted that for the projection year of 1980, Olsen and Westley indicated a rise in truck operating speed. For level terrain and congested conditions, speeds on freeways, multilane highways, and two-lane highways have been calculated at 45.6, 39.2, and 34.0 mph, respectively. The speeds used in our study have been assumed to remain constant.

A scattergram with DOT travel time on the y axis and

airline travel time on the x axis was plotted. A strong linear relationship was observed. These 29 links were then regressed to the times of the NJDOT data and the following equation resulted:

$$Y=1.5X-0.65 \qquad (1)$$

where   Y=one-way travel time in minutes from DOT data;

X=one-way travel time in minutes as the crow flies, assuming different truck speeds along different routes.

The standard error of the estimate was 3.4 minutes, the r value was .961.

Next, airline distance in miles was regressed against DOT travel times without assuming different truck speeds. The fit was slightly less satisfactory with an r of .922 and a standard error of the estimate of 4.75 minutes.

$$Y=2.2 \ X_m-.91 \qquad (2)$$

where   Y=one-way travel time in minutes from DOT data;

X_m=airline distance in miles.

It was concluded that even though the method for cal-culating the speed of the garbage trucks was imprecise, it probably mirrored fact pretty well. If other measurements for capacity restraints such as traffic volumes and signals had been available, we assumed that the standard error could have been further reduced.

The sources and sinks of the system were located on the computer map. A ruler distance was measured for all the links. These distances became the X values in equation (1) above and a series of Y values representing travel times was obtained for all the links.

SELECTION OF IMPORTANT PATHS FOR INCORPORATION INTO THE MODEL

The choice of links for inclusion in the model runs is a critical step. The analyst must decide if the added com-puter and labor costs are worth the possible information to be gained from including all or most of the possible links. On the one hand, we have seen optimization studies in which the results were, in essence, predetermined because so few alternatives were available. For example, a solid waste study which is programmed for 25 sources and 45 links probably does not warrant a modeling effort of the kind developed in this volume. On the other hand, a system of 25 sources and 300 links will be informative, but will also be extremely expensive to run. If the analyst has unlimited computer time and a large staff, then an 800-link system can be modeled. Few studies are so well endowed.

In the case at hand, our system potentially had 719 links (Exhibit 5.1).

The 719 potential links were reduced to 319 links (Exhibit 5.2). In order to recognize the legal responsibility of the Meadowlands region to accept the waste from most of the communities in the five-county study area, every source was linked to at least one Meadowlands facility of each type: existing-landfill, dry fuel, and gas pyrolysis.

Second, every source was given links to at least two facilities of each type. A few waste sheds were given four links.

The precise selection of links to choose other than Meadowlands links was made on the basis of geography, tempered by political reality. The geographical consideration was cost minimization for the hauler. For example, preliminary calculations of transportation costs indicated that it was not necessary to link central and northern Bergen County communities to landfills or recovery facilities in the southern portion of the study area (Middlesex, Somerset, and Union counties). Likewise, we did not link waste sheds in the southern portion of the study area to sites in central and northern Bergen County. It makes little sense to link a community to a facility 30 miles away when the same facility or facilities are available 10 miles away. The possibility that county solutions to the management problem may be feasible led us to choose at least one link in the county, wherever possible. The county assignments were nearly always the minimum cost link.

The summary of 319 links (Exhibit 5.2) indicates that each waste shed was assigned between 9 and 14 links. The two extreme cases, waste sheds 6 and 22, may be used to illustrate the link selection process. Waste shed 6 lies in east-central Bergen County. The closest destinations for its solid waste are the Bergen County landfills; the non-Bergen County, Meadowlands landfills; and any recovery facilities that might be developed in the Meadowlands or

EXHIBIT 5.1

POTENTIAL LINKS IN THE
SOLID WASTE MANAGEMENT MODEL

From	*To*	*Number of Possible Links*
25 waste sheds	6 existing landfills	150
25 waste sheds	7 proposed landfills	175
25 waste sheds	7 dry fuel facilities	175
25 waste sheds	4 gas pyrolysis facilities	100
7 dry fuel facilities	7 electric generating stations	49
7 dry fuel facilities	6 existing landfills	42
4 gas pyrolysis facilities	7 electric generating stations	28

Total Potential Links	719

EXHIBIT 5.2

SUMMARY: LINKS INCLUDED IN THE ANALYSIS

Waste Shed		Existing Landfills	Proposed Landfills	Dry Fuel Facilities	Gas Pyrolysis Facilities	Generating Plants	Total Links
Bergen	1	3	2	4	2	0	11
County	2	3	2	3	2	0	10
	3	3	2	3	2	0	10
	4	3	2	3	2	0	10
	5	2	3	4	2	0	11
	6	2	2	3	2	0	9
	7	2	3	4	2	0	11
	8	2	3	3	2	0	10
Hudson	9	2	3	4	2	0	11
County	10	2	3	4	2	0	11
Passaic	11	3	3	4	2	0	12
County	12	2	3	3	2	0	10
	13	2	4	3	2	0	11
	14	2	3	4	2	0	11
	15	3	2	4	2	0	11
Essex	16	2	2	4	2	0	10
County	17	4	3	3	2	0	12
	18	3	3	3	3	0	12
	19	3	3	3	2	0	11
	20	4	5	2	2	0	13
Union	21	3	4	3	3	0	13
County	22	4	3	4	3	0	14
	23	4	3	3	3	0	13
	24	4	3	3	2	0	12
	25	4	3	2	2	0	11
7 Dry Fuel Fac.		8	0	0	0	27	35
4 Gas Pyr. Fac.		0	0	0	0	4	4
Total Links		79	72	83	54	31	319

central Bergen County. Overall, source no. 6's choices are
limited to only the south and the west.

In contrast, waste shed 22 has reasonable choices to
the north, south, east, and west. To the north are the
Meadowlands and possible Newark facilities, to the east
are proposed sites in Elizabeth and Linden. And landfill
sites lie to the south in Middlesex County and to the west
in Morris County. Overall, the more centrally located
waste sheds were assigned more links than the peripheral
sheds.

The intermediate-to-final facility links were chosen
to minimize cost. In the case of the dry fuel system, the
amount of recovered energy assigned to a particular electric generating station was constrained. Therefore, multiple links to electric generating stations were assigned.
With one exception, all the residue from the dry fuel plants
was sent to the Meadowlands. The one exception is the
Elizabeth facility, which was given the option of the Meadowlands or the Edison landfills. Each of the gas pyrolysis
facilities was linked to a single electric generating station in recognition of the high costs of moving this energy
product.

ESTIMATION OF TRANSPORTATION COSTS VIA
DIRECT HAUL AND WITH TRANSFER STATIONS

Given a set of 319 transportation links, we estimated
the cost of moving the waste along 315 of these links by
direct truck haul and sometimes with a transfer station.
The four cost estimates for moving the gas recovered by the
pyrolysis process are reviewed in Chapter 7.

Direct-Haul Costs

Our review of local conditions and the literature iso-
lated six possible direct-haul modes involving different
truck sizes and crew sizes. Municipal collection systems
rely to a large extent on 20-cubic-yard collection vehicles
and to a lesser degree on smaller 18-cubic-yard vehicles.
For example, in Middlesex and Union counties, New Jersey,
more than three-fourths of the municipal collection vehicles are of the 20-cubic-yard size. Only 8 percent use the
large 25-cubic-yard trucks. Conversely, more than half the
private collection firms use the larger 25-cubic-yard-capa-
city vehicles. Forty percent use 20-cubic-yard trucks.
Only 10 percent use small trucks.

EXHIBIT 5.3

COSTS FOR SELECTED DIRECT-HAUL
REAR-LOADING VEHICLES, 1974[a]
($1,000s)

Size in cubic yards	Cost Range[b]	Unit Costs	Annual Costs[c]
18	18-25	22.5	5.445
20	19-28	26.0	6.292
25	24-32	28.5	6.897

[a]All estimates exclude the cost of tires, which may add $900 to $2,000 to the price of a vehicle, depending on the type, size, and number of tires required.

[b]Estimated cost ranges are based on a review of manufacturers' listed prices conducted in 1973-74 by the staff of the Middlesex County Solid Waste Management Program.

[c]Assumes an average amortization rate of 7 percent for five years for collection vehicles.

EXHIBIT 5.4

ESTIMATED AVERAGE PAYLOADS FOR
SELECTED REFUSE COLLECTION VEHICLES, 1974

Size in Cubic Yards	Compaction[a] Efficiency (lbs/cubic yard)	Estimated Payloads (tons)	Average Payloads (tons)
18	450-500	4.0-5.0	4.25
20	450-550	4.5-5.5	5.00
25	500-650	6.25-8.0	7.00

[a]Compaction efficiency based on a review of manufacturers'
literature and information provided by municipal and private vehicle collectors in Middlesex County, N.J.

By 1980 we expect the present pattern to change in the
direction of larger trucks. Generally, private carters
amortize equipment more rapidly (three to five years) than
their municipal counterparts (10 years) and replace equipment more frequently. Private firms appear to select the
more efficient 25-cubic-yard trucks to replace older equipment. Therefore, in modeling the municipal solid waste
system for 1980 and 1985, we have assumed that private
haulers will be using 25-cubic-yard trucks.

Municipal waste collection agencies replace collection
vehicles less frequently because of the difficulties they
face in obtaining appropriations for routine vehicle replacement. As a result they tend to operate older and
smaller trucks, many more than ten years old. While recent
purchases of new equipment by municipal agencies have
tended to be of the 25-cubic-yard type, we have assumed that
by 1980 the modal vehicle unit for the municipal agencies
will be 20 cubic yards.

The equipment cost implications of this choice are
illustrated in Exhibit 5.3. The 25-cubic-yard trucks cost
more than the smaller vehicles. However, they more than
compensate for the added 10 to 25 percent cost by being
more efficient. The 25-cubic-yard trucks have much higher
average payloads than their smaller counterparts (Exhibit
5.4). Average payloads for 18-cubic-yard vehicles in the
study area tend to be below average because the majority
are older and less efficient than new equipment. Many
municipalities reserve these relatively small vehicles for
special collections and as backup equipment. Average payloads for the larger, 25-cubic-yard vehicles are closer to
the maximum reported payloads. The average has been chosen
to compensate for less intensively used municipal equipment.
Overall, the 40 percent to 65 percent payload advantage of
the large truck can reduce the number of trips and/or trucks
required by a community.

The other major choice we observed is crew size. Our
review suggests that private contractors tend to use a combination of large truck and two-man crew, while the municipal agencies use smaller trucks and three-man crews. The
additional crew man further increases the unit cost of the
municipal operations.

The six cost combinations of two crew sizes and three
truck sizes are listed in Exhibit 5.5. The least expensive
combination is the two-man crew/18-cubic-yard truck; the
most expensive is the three-man crew/25-cubic-yard vehicle.
The 20-cubic-yard truck/three-man crew combination for the

EXHIBIT 5.5

ESTIMATED COSTS FOR ALTERNATIVE
CREW-SIZE AND VEHICLE-SIZE OPERATIONS

All Costs in 1974 dollars

Truck Size and Crew Size

Cost Category	18 cubic yard		20 cubic yard		25 cubic yard	
	2-man	3-man	2-man	3-man	2-man	3-man
EQUIPMENT[a] *Total*	10,500	10,500	11,692	11,692	13,150	13,150
Vehicle Depreciation	5,450	5,450	6,292	6,292	6,900	6,900
Maintenance and Repair	2,250	2,250	2,600	2,600	2,850	2,850
Consumable Items	2,800	2,800	2,800	2,800	3,400	3,400
LABOR[b] *Total*	25,667	38,278	25,667	38,278	25,667	38,278
Salaries and Wages	19,015	28,355	19,015	28,355	19,015	28,355
Fringe Benefits	3,800	5,670	3,800	5,670	3,800	5,670
Overtime	2,852	4,253	2,852	4,253	2,852	4,253
ADMINISTRATION AND OTHER[c] *Total*	7,200	8,600	7,200	8,600	7,200	8,600
Supervision and Management	2,850	4,250	2,850	4,250	2,850	4,250
Insurance and Legal	1,200	1,200	1,200	1,200	1,200	1,200
Licenses and Fees	750	750	750	750	750	750
Other Fixed Overhead	2,400	2,400	2,400	2,400	2,400	2,400
TOTAL ANNUAL COST	43,367	57,378	44,562	58,570	46,017	60,028
COST PER MINUTE	0.36	0.48	0.37	0.49	0.38	0.50
COST PER TON/PER MINUTE	0.84	.113	.074	.098	.054	.071

[a]__Equipment Costs__. Vehicle depreciation-amortization for five years at 7 percent interest. Maintenance and repair: 10 percent of initial vehicle cost 5-7 cents per mile for 40,000 miles per year. __Consumable Items__: tires: one set per year at $150 per tire, fuel: $.40/gallon, assuming 20,000 miles per year and five miles per gallon, Oil: $300.00 (150 quarts at $2.00 per quart).

EXHIBIT 5.5 (continued)

ESTIMATED COSTS FOR ALTERNATIVE CREW-SIZE AND
VEHICLE-SIZE OPERATIONS

---

[b]
Labor Costs. Salaries and wages: average annual salary of $9,675 for drivers
and $9,340 for loaders based on recent contracts in the region, Fringe benefits:
20 percent of salaries and wages, Overtime: 15 percent of salaries and wages.

[c]
Administration and Other Expenses. Supervision and management: 15 percent
of salaries and wages, Insurance: $100.00 per month, Licenses and fees:
$750.00 per year.

Source: The source of these data is the Middlesex County Solid Waste Program.

modal municipal agency is 27 percent more expensive than
the two-man crew/25-cubic-yard truck combination for the
modal private contractor.

The difference between the two modal groups is increased
when the greater efficiency of the 25-cubic-yard truck is
taken into account. Specifically, the difference increases
to 81 percent (Exhibit 5.5, last row) when the annual costs
are divided by the amount of operational time of the truck
crew (about 120,000 minutes per year) and the average payloads of the trucks (Exhibit 5.4). It is this cost-per-
ton-per-minute figure which is the critical transportation
cost variable.

Direct-haul transportation costs were developed for all
315 links in two stages. First, we had to establish the
haul cost per ton per minute for each of the 25 waste sheds.
Towns were phoned to establish whether they were served
by private carters or by municipal agencies. Pure cases
(an entire waste shed served by either a municipal or a
private carter) were assigned either a $.098 per-ton-per-
minute (municipal) or a $.054 per-ton-per-minute (private)
cost. Most of the waste sheds had some communities served
by municipal agencies and others by private contractors.
In those mixed cases, a per-ton-per-minute cost was calculated by weighing the modal cost ($.098 or $.054) by each
community's population (a measure of waste generation).
Summarizing, each of the mixed-case waste sheds was assigned
transportation costs between $.098 and $.054 per ton per
minute. The average direct-haul transportation cost used
in the study is $.067 per ton per minute and the range is
$.098 to $.054.

The final direct-haul cost estimates were obtained by
multiplying the per-ton-per-minute cost for each waste
shed by two times the one-way travel time in minutes plus
a 20-minute turn-around time.

TRANSFER STATIONS

Transfer stations can produce significant savings when
a large amount of waste is to be hauled long distances. On
the other hand, transfer stations are an expense added to
the already high cost of waste disposal. Briefly, a transfer station is a fixed facility at which waste is transferred from small vehicles (18 to 25 cubic yards) to larger
(65 cubic yard) trucks or rail cars. The facility, which
usually covers about five acres, contains storage areas,
scales for weighing the waste, and compactors for reducing
its volume.

Cost estimates for operating a transfer station vary
with facility size. Small facilities (150 tons per day)
are more expensive to operate per unit of waste than large
facilities (500 tons per day).

A review of local conditions led us to select 250 tons
per day as a modular planning unit for a transfer station.
The costs of operating a 250-ton-per-day facility is dis-
played as annual facility costs (Exhibit 5.6) and as annual
transportation and time-related costs (Exhibit 5.7).

The combination of the constant $1.93-per-ton station
operating cost and $.024-per-ton-per-minute transportation
cost was measured against the direct-haul transportation
costs discussed above (Exhibit 5.5). Specifically, the $.024-
per-ton-per-minute transportation cost was multiplied by
two times the one-way travel time plus a 50-minute turn-
around time. The $1.93 was added to derive a total trans-
portation cost per ton for all 315 links.

Four classes of waste sources may be distinguished with
respect to the feasibility of transfer station use. First,
all the dry fuel facility link costs to electric generating
stations or to landfills were based on the $.024-per-ton-per-
minute estimate derived in Exhibit 5.7. Second, four of the 25
waste sheds already have transfer stations. In these cases,
a link-by-link evaluation was made to determine if the transfer station reduced the haul cost. In almost every case
the transfer station did indeed reduce the haul cost. In
such cases the transfer station was used for all the model
runs.

A third set of waste sheds exceed the 250-ton-per-day
waste-generation threshold required for the establishment
of a single transfer station. A fourth set of waste sheds
do not generate the required 250 tons per day to warrant a
transfer station. In these cases, we evaluated transfer
stations for 1980 or 1985 if the waste shed passed the 250-
ton-per-day threshold. The reader should note that few of
the communities in the study area generate enough waste to
warrant a transfer station individually. Our analysis of
transfer stations at the waste-shed level assumes that
communities will recognize the possible economic advantages
of transfer stations.

The final decision to develop new transfer station capacity
was made on a link-by-link basis. The direct-haul cost was
compared with a haul cost assuming a transfer station. If
the cost of direct haul was 50 percent greater than the cost
of haul with a transfer station, then transfer station cost
links were established. The decision to use a 50 percent
added cost threshold reflects our judgment that unless major

EXHIBIT 5.6

ESTIMATED ANNUAL COST OF A 250-TON PER DAY TRANSFER STATION, EXCLUDING COSTS ASSOCIATED WITH MILEAGE AND TIME

(75,000 tons per year)

1974 dollars

Item	Dollar Cost
FIXED [a]	37,300
Salaries and Wages	
One supervisor	15,000
One laborer	11,500
Insurance and Legal	3,000
Accounting	2,000
Licenses and Fees	500
Management and Administration	5,300
VARIABLE [a]	43,675
Maintenance and Repair	25,925
Supplies	1,200
Utilities (less electric power)	3,600
Electric Power	12,000
Uniforms and Laundry	950
CAPITAL CHARGES [b]	64,025
Land and Building	
(@ 6 percent for 20 years)	25,285
Station Equipment	
(@ 6 percent for 10 years)	10,190
Other Capital Costs	28,550
TOTAL ANNUAL OPERATING COSTS	145,000
TOTAL ANNUAL OPERATING COST PER TON	$1.93

[a] Estimated in a manner similar to Exhibit 5.5

[b] Land and building costs: Includes general site preparation, grading, paving access roads and parking areas, landscaping, fencing and lighting. Assumes 5 acres of land at $30,000 per acre, estimated building size of 50' by 80' (4000 square feet @ $35 per square foot) which includes floor area need for one-day storage of refuse, plus a push

EXHIBIT 5.6 (continued)

ESTIMATED ANNUAL COST OF A 250-TON PER DAY
TRANSFER STATION, EXCLUDING COSTS ASSOCIATED
WITH MILEAGE AND TIME

---

pit, compaction equipment, and office space. Station equipment
costs: includes stationary compactor and hopper, one pit, and
one truck scale. See the Heil Company, A Handbook for Transfer
Systems Analysis (Milwaukee, Wis.: Heil Company, 1974 and Disko
1974, p.334, for specific numbers, types and costs of equipment recommended for various size transfer stations. Other capital costs:
Includes engineering design and construction supervision estimated
here at 12 percent of total fixed capital and a contingency fund
for facility startup and emergency repairs or modification. The
second charge is assumed to be equal to four months' gross
operating costs or 10 percent of total fixed capital which-
ever is greater.

EXHIBIT 5.7

ESTIMATED ANNUAL COST FOR TRANSFER VEHICLE AND OPERATIONS
1974 Dollars

	Item	Dollar Cost
TIME-BASED TRANSPORT COSTS	Total	$27,985
Amortization of Transfer Trailer [a]		3,288
Amortization of Transfer Tractor [a]		4,027
Labor Costs[b]		12,600
Administrative and Other[c]		8,070
MILEAGE-BASED TRANSPORTATION COSTS	Total	13,450
Maintenance and Repair [d]		4,450
Total Consumables [e]		9,000
TOTAL ANNUAL COSTS		41,435
COST PER TON PER MINUTE[f]		.024

[a]Assumes an average amortization period of eight years for both transfer trailer and tractor at 7 percent interest. Four 65-cubic-yard transfer trailers ($20,000 each) are assumed for each 250 ton-per-day facility. Three diesel tractors ($24,500 each) are assumed for each 250 ton per day facility.

[b]Includes salaries and wages, fringe benefits estimated at 20 percent of direct wages and salaries for such items as retirement, medical insurance, union dues, workman's compensation, insurance premiums, and social security. Overtime charges have not been included. However, some overtime charges may be incurred to compensate for equipment down-time or to replace temporarily unavilable equipment.

[c]Includes supervision and management, insurance and legal costs, licenses, and fees. Supervision support costs estimated at 20 percent of direct salaries and wages. Insurance and legal costs estimated as $200 per month per vehicle.

[d]Assumes approximately 10 percent of the initial vehicle cost per year or about 10-11 cents per mile for 40,000 miles per year.

[e]Consumable items include fuel, oil, and tires. Diesel fuel estimated at $.40 per gallon, 5 miles per gallon, and 40,000 miles per year; oil for lubrication and for the hydraulic system estimated at 200 quarts per year at $2 per quart; tires assume one complete set of 20 replacement tires per year at $150 per tire.

EXHIBIT 5.7

ESTIMATED ANNUAL COST FOR TRANSFER VEHICLE AND OPERATIONS
1974 Dollars

_fAssumes 112,320 minutes per year available for the time-based transport costs; 80,000 minutes for the mileage-based transport costs. Therefore, $27,985 per 112,320 minutes = $.25 per minute and $13,450 per 80,000 minutes = $.17 per minute. Adding $.25 per minute + $0.17 per minute = $.42 per minute. The payload capacity of the vehicle is estimated to be 17.5 tons. Dividing $.42 per minute by 17.5 tons = $.024 per ton per minute.

savings are apparent few communities will be willing to
raise capital funds for a transfer station to be jointly
operated with neighboring communities. Frankly, conversations with decision-makers in some communities lead us to
conclude that perhaps the 50 percent ratio is not high
enough.

Overall, transfer station decisions were made on a link-
by-link basis for the 280 source-to-intermediate-or-final
facility links. Only existing transfer station links were
incorporated in the 1975 runs. The 71 transfer station
links are summarized in Exhibit 5.8.

EXHIBIT 5.8

SUMMARY OF SYSTEM LINKS WHICH
ASSUME TRANSFER STATIONS, 1975-1985

Transportation Links	*1975*	*1980*	*1985*	*Percent of Total Links 1985*
Links to Landfill Sites	26	49	52	34
Links to Resource Recovery Sites	0	19	19	14
Total	26	68	71	25

The results are extremely revealing. One-third of the
source-to-landfill links can profit from a transfer station
by 1985, while only 14 percent of the links-to-recovery
sites can benefit economically from a transfer facility.
All 19 links from sources to recovery facilities which
warrant a transfer station are associated with already existing stations. No new transfer stations from waste sheds
to our proposed recovery facilities are warranted.

Three reasons account for this important finding. First,
many of the waste sheds which face a long haul to Meadowlands or to other recovery facilities do not generate enough
waste to meet the 250-ton-per-day transfer station
threshold. Smaller 150-ton-per-day stations might have
made a facility possible in several of these communities.

Second, our assumption that individual communities would
not be able or willing to raise the funds for community or
regional transfer stations unless they found out that their

EXHIBIT 5.9

SOURCE AND DESTINATION OF POTENTIAL, NEW
TRANSFER STATION LINKS, 1975-1985

Destination of Waste	County Origin of Waste					Total Links
	Bergen	Hudson	Passaic	Essex	Union	
Edison	2	2	0	3	0	7
Fairfield	1	1	0	1	0	3
Hanover	0	1	0	1	0	2
Totowa	0	1	0	1	0	2
Mount Olive	1	0	0	0	1	2
Madison	0	0	0	3	0	3
Chester	0	0	0	2	1	3
South Brunswick	0	0	0	1	1	2
Bridgewater	0	0	0	1	1	2
Total Links	4	5	0	13	4	26

community was paying 50 percent more for direct haul than haul with a transfer station prevented the development of transfer station links. In short, the use of the 250-ton-per-day threshold and 1.50 savings ratio to reflect economic and political realities temper the conclusion that transfer stations are not needed in combination with resource recovery facilities.

Third, the location of the dispersed resource recovery facilities is probably the most important factor explaining the apparent rejection of combination transfer station resource recovery links on economic grounds. Specifically, we deliberately located facilities with county units in mind in order to recognize the potential political importance of county units and to reduce the haul time. These dispersed sites made transfer stations unnecessary.

The critical significance of the long trip length versus fixed charge of $1.93 per ton tradeoff in the hauling option is clearly illustrated by the 26 new transfer station links added to move solid waste from sources to landfills between 1975 and 1985 (Exhibit 5.9). Twenty-two of the 26 proposed transfer-station-to-landfill links are to landfills outside the five county Meadowlands source area. Seven are to the large Middlesex County landfills along the Raritan River from such densely populated communities as Newark and Jersey City. These seven links, the two links to Mount Olive, the three to Madison, and the three to Chester are a clear indication of future regional solid waste trip patterns if the disposal price in the Meadowlands is increased. To the hauler, a transfer station may be a better choice than a shorter haul to a facility which imposes a high landfill charge.

Summarizing, this chapter has developed a methodology for calculating the transportation costs along 315 paths from sources to intermediate facilities and final sites, and from intermediate facilities to final sites. The choice of links from this matrix of potential paths is the focus of Chapter 8.

NOTES

1. R. J. Paquette, Transportation Engineering (New York: Ronald Press, 1972), p. 337.

2. B. M. Martin, F. W. Memmott, III, and A. J. Bone, Principles and Techniques of Predicting Future Demand for Urban Area Transportation (Cambridge, Mass.: M.I.T. Press, 1961), p. 30.

3. J. B. Garner and D. R. Parsons, "Measuring Journey Speeds and Flows," Highway Research Record, no. 456 (1973), p. 3.

4. C. Haley, E. Hall, and A. Johnson, "Travel Time--A Measure of Service and a Criterion for Improvement Priorities," Highway Research Record, no. 35 (1963), p. 1.

5. Garner and Parsons, op. cit., pp. 2-4.

6. G. R. Wells, Traffic Engineering (London: Charles Griffin and Company, 1970), pp. 39-41, and M. J. Bruton, Introduction to Transportation Planning (London: Hutchinson Technical Education, 1970), pp. 62-63.

7. See note 3, above, for reference.

8. Chicago Area Transportation Study, Vols. I, II, III (Chicago: Department of Commerce, Bureau of Public Roads, 1962).

9. Martin, et al., op. cit., p. 82.

10. R. Smock, "A Comparative Description of a Capacity-Restrained Traffic Assignment," Highway Research Record, no. 6 (1963), pp. 14-15.

11. A. Benesh, "Traffic Assignment without Bias," Highway Research Record, no. 392 (1972), pp. 36-46.

12. P. M. Dalton and H. M. Harmelink, "Development and Testing of a Multipath--Assignment Technique," Highway Research Record, no. 392 (1972), pp. 136-138.

13. Edwards and Kelsey, Inc., Transportation Operations: Program to Improve Capacity and Safety for the County of Morris (Newark, N.J.: Edwards and Kelsey, Inc. 1972), pp. 35-39.

14.   G. J. Brown and A. H. Woehrle, Jr., "Program, Inputs and Calibration of the Direct Traffic Estimation Method," Highway Research Record, no. 250 (1968), pp. 18-24.

15.   R. Creighton, Urban Transportation Planning (Urbana, Ill.:   University of Illinois Press, 1970), p. 166.

16.   R. J. Olsen and G. W. Westley, Synthetic Measures of Truck Operating Times between the Metropolitan Centers of BEA Economic Areas: 1950, 1960, 1970, with Projections for 1980 (Oak Ridge, Tenn.:   Oak Ridge National Laboratory, January 1975).

CHAPTER 6

THE MARKETS FOR MATERIALS
RECOVERED FROM SOLID WASTE

This chapter will attempt to identify existing and potential markets through 1985 for the types of materials to be recovered in the various solid waste processing alternatives explored in this book. General materials and price trends will be analyzed. Price ranges will be estimated in 1974 dollars.[1] The price estimates are intentionally conservative in recognition of their characteristic unpredictability and the dependence of the processing options on a materials cash flow.

PROJECTED RECOVERY MIXES

The following section reviews the projected recovery mixes for a maximum recovery strategy for all waste generated in 1980 and 1985 in the five-county study area. It is not definite or even likely that all of the region's waste will be channeled into such extensive materials recovery processing. It is clear that at least some reclamation of ferrous metal and paper is likely in the near future. The analysis is limited to those commodities for which the technology and marketing have been successfully demonstrated on a commercial scale at this time (Exhibits 6.1 and 6.2). Hence dry or wet separation of paper, and recovery of other nonferrous metal, has been omitted, although these will most probably be feasible by 1985 and can be added onto existing recovery modules.

Newspaper, corrugate, and other paper such as carefully controlled or mixed office waste, are primarily to be recovered at the local level by governments, businesses, and private scavengers at the source, enabling the paper to be recovered as distinct products and to be relatively contaminant-free. Thirty to 40 percent of the paper in our waste stream could be recovered as a fiber source through source separation. A Midwest Research Institute report pinpoints the maximum post-consumer recovery potential for Standard Metropolitan Statistical Areas (SMSAs) as 40 percent.[2] This is derived from the following post-consumer recovery rates for the four major components of the waste-paper stream: (1) used news, 43 percent; (2) used corrugate, 35 percent; (3) mixed papers, 39 percent;[3] and (4) high-grade deinking II (carefully separated office writing and bond papers only), 11 percent. The estimated maximum recovery ranges are 40 to 50 percent for used newspapers, 45 to 55 percent for used corrugate, for high-grade deinking II, 10 to 16 percent and 35 to 45 percent for mixed papers.[4] Since the source separation rates for the paper components in the projected mix are not the maximums feasible, an additional 15 percent of the total waste news and 15 percent of the total corrugated (7 percent of the paper) is assumed to be recovered by handpicking at the recovery site.

With the exception of aluminum, no source separation of other components is assumed. Light and other ferrous metal are assumed to be separated by means of an air knife for marketing purposes. The light ferrous, consisting primarily of cans, needs to be detinned before marketing as scrap; the heavy fraction can be marketed as is. Although a 90 percent recovery coefficient is employed here, estimates of feasible ferrous recovery range up to 98 percent of the content in the waste input. Glass recovery is approximately 60 percent for cullet, 80 percent for fines; the average used here is 70 percent. Aluminum recovery by heavy media is estimated at 80 percent by the National Center for Resource Recovery. Combustion Power Company, applying aluminum magnet separation of the can stock only, reports a recovery rate of 84 percent, or 54 percent overall, in initial testing, which will most likely improve with future applications.[5]

The refuse-derived fuel, or air classified light fraction containing no more than 10 percent moisture on a dry-weight basis, can be marketed as is. These figures assume conversion to pyrolytic oil, gas, or steam fuel sources. This quantity of waste would produce 29,860 barrels of oil, or one per ton of generated (initial RDF. An ultimated residue from both the heavies of the refuse and energy

recovery residue is shown in the two exhibits. Overall,
Exhibits 6.1 and 6.2 assume a recovery strategy aimed at
materials rather than energy recovery.

THE REGIONAL AND NATIONAL MATERIALS OUTLOOK

In 1972 an average of more than 20 tons of basic minerals and nonfood organic materials worth more than $200
was consumed on a per-capita basis in the United States
(Exhibit 6.3). On a weight basis, the nonmetallic minerals
and fuels stand out and on a value basis the fossil fuels
predominate. Net imports of many of these basic products
are sizable and are projected to increase (Exhibit 6.4).

In its special report on materials in short supply,
the Department of Commerce discusses the chronic concern of
industrial nations (illustrated by Exhibits 6.3 and 6.4):
the adequacy of accessible natural resources for meeting
near-term and long-term needs. The Commerce Department
lists 29 commodities which were in short supply in 1974,
among them major sources of secondary materials and their
virgin counterparts.[6] The department sees shortages as increasingly more common, with the short-term "solution" of
sharp price rises,and consequent frustration of business conditions with possible unemployment and bankruptcy. The
Port Authority of New York and New Jersey reported in January
1974 that energy and basic commodity shortages had been in-
strumental in bringing about a depressed regional economy
in 1974 and thereafter.[7]

According to the Commerce Department, shortages of primary materials have been generated and accentuated by (1)
the realignment of dollar exchange rates with respect to
foreign currencies in December 1971 and February 1973, which
likewise favored the export of foods and inputs such as
hides, softwood logs, phosphates, and scrap metals; (2) the
interruption of Mideast petroleum shipments in late 1973;
and (3) the sharp increase in prices charged for bauxite,
petroleum products, and primary metals by countries owning
the world's choicest supplies.[8]

In its Second Report to Congress on Resource Recovery
(1974), the Environmental Protection Agency stated that in
the absence of technological, economic, and institutional
constraints, municipal waste could generate 4 to 5 million
barrels of oil a day, or 1 percent of United States annual
needs, and meet the following percentages of our annual
national demands: iron, 7 percent; aluminum, 8 percent; tin,
20 percent; and paper, 14 percent. The National Commission

EXHIBIT 6.1

PROJECTED RECOVERY MIX FOR TOTAL REFUSE, 1980

3,270,200 tons/year [a]
  62,892 tons/week
  55,659 tons/week Input to Resource Recovery

Component	Total Refuse %	Total Refuse TPW g	Source Separation %	Source Separation TPW g	Resource Recovery %(of total)	Resource Recovery TPW g	Total Recovery %	Total Recovery TPW g
PAPER	33.2	20,881	29.2	6,101	6.9 [b]	1,444	36.1	7,545
Newsprint	6.6	4,151	40.0	1,660	15.0	623	55.0	2,283
Corrugate	8.7	5,472	40.0	2,189	15.0	821	55.0	3,010
Other Paper	17.9	11,258	20.0	2,252			20.0	2,252
FERROUS METAL	7.7	4,843			90.0	4,359	90.0	3,892 [c]
Light (65%)	5.0	3,145				2,831		2,527
Heavy (35%)	2.7	1,698				1,528		1,365
GLASS	9.4	5,912			70.0	4,138	70.0	4,138
ALUMINUM	.6	377	9.5 [d]	36	65.0	212	74.5	248
OTHER REFUSE	26.6	16,728						
MOISTURE (20-25%)	22.5	14,151	8.0	1,132	71.0	10,047	79.0	11,179
TOTAL	100.0	62,892	11.5	7,269	32.3	20,200	43.3	27,002
REFUSE DERIVED FUELS [e]							45.4	28,367 [f]
RESIDUE							11.3	7,059 [f]
TOTAL							100.0	62,428

[a]Assumes a 1980 population of 3,657,117 at 4.9 lbs. per-capita/day. Compositional array - Source: NCRR National Survey 1968-Waste as Generated.
[b]The percent in the paper category pertains to handpicking at the recovery site. The remainder are technical coefficients for materials processing.
[c]Here ferrous is in gross tons. Net ton equivalents in previous column.

EXHIBIT 6.1 (continued)

PROJECTED RECOVERY MIX FOR TOTAL REFUSE, 1980

---

dAssumes 15 percent source separation can stock which is approximately 64 percent of total aluminum.

eAir classified material to be used as dry fuel or input into pyrolysis or other energy recovery systems, e.g., one barrel pyrolytic oil per ton of RDF.

fAfter 5 percent of residue generated in energy recovery is transferred to total residue. Initial RDF was 29,860 and initial residue after material recovery was 5,566.

gTPW is tons per week.

EXHIBIT 6.2

PROJECTED RECOVERY MIX FOR TOTAL REFUSE, 1985

4,025,168.5 tons per year a
   77,407 tons per week
   68,510 tons per week Input to Resource Recovery

Component	Total Refuse %	TPW	Source Separation %	TPW	Resource Recovery %(of total)	TPW	Total Recovery %	TPW
PAPER	33.2	25,699	29.2	7,504	6.9	1,773	36.1	9,285
Newspaper	6.6	5,109	40.0	2,044	15.0	766	55.0	2,810
Corrugate	8.7	6,734	40.0	2,694	·15.0	1,010	55.0	3,704
Other Paper	17.9	13,856	20.0	2,771			20.0	2,771
FERROUS METAL	7.7	5,960			90.0	5,364	90.0	4,789 b
Light (65%)	5.0	3,870				3,483		3,110
Heavy (35%)	2.7	2,090				1,881		1,679
GLASS	9.4	7,276			70.0	5,093	70.0	5,093
ALUMINUM	.6	464	9.5	44	65.0	273	65.0	317
OTHER REFUSE	26.6	20,590						
MOISTURE(20-25%)	22.5	17,418	8.0	1,393	71.0	12,367	79.0	13,760
TOTAL	100.0	77,407	11.5	8,941	32.2	24,870	43.3	33,244
REFUSE-DERIVED FUEL							45.5	34,941
RESIDUE							11.2	8,670
TOTAL							100.0	76,855

[a]Assumes a 1985 population of 3,803,710 at 5.8 pounds per-capita day. Compositional array source: NCRR National Survey 1968-Waste as Generated.

[b]Here Ferrous Metal is in Gross Tons. Net Ton equivalents in previous column.

EXHIBIT 6.3

VALUE AND WEIGHT OF RAW MATERIALS USED PER CAPITA
IN THE UNITED STATES, 1972

Raw Material	Weight, Pounds	Per Capita Value, Dollars
Fossil Fuels	17,800	121.14
Petroleum	7,800	85.10
Coal	5,000	17.07
Natural Gas	5,000	18.97
Nonmetallic Minerals	20,550	22.45
Sand and Gravel	9,000	5.47
Stone	8,500	5.94
Other	3,050	11.04
Metals	1,340	55.95
Iron and Steel	1,200	24.43
Other	140	31.02
Forest Products	2,810	36.40
Total Weight Raw Materials	42,500	235.94

Source: National Commission on Materials Policy, Material
Needs and the Environment Today and Tomorrow,
final report, (Washington, D.C.: U. S. Government
Printing Office, June 1973).

EXHIBIT 6.4

NET IMPORTS AS A PROPORTION OF DOMESTIC USE IN THE UNITED STATES 1970

Ferrous Metals		*Nonferrous Metals*		*Other Basic Materials*	
Iron Ore	30% [a]	Aluminum (bauxite)	86	Petroleum	22
Chromium	100	Beryllium	w	Natural Gas	3
Cobalt	96	Copper	8	Uranium	0
Columbium	100	Lead	40	Timber Products	8[b]
Manganese	94	Magnesium	0	Natural Rubber	100
Nickel	91	Mercury	38		
Tungsten	w	Platinum	98		
Vanadium	1	Tin	100		
		Titanium	47		
w - withheld		Zinc	60		

[a]By 1985 iron ore impacts are expected to rise to 50% as are imports of lead and tungsten.   Source: Institute of Scrap Iron & Steel, Phoenix Quarterly, Vol. 6, No. 1, Spring 1974.

[b]Net imports in 1972 are up 50% from 1970.

Source: National Commission on Materials Policy, Interim Report (Washington, D.C.:   U.S. Government Printing Office, April 1972).

on Materials Policy found that use of the aluminium, steel, and paper available from municipal waste in lieu of primary sources by the respective industries would save an additional 386 billion KWH, or 2 percent of the energy demand. [9]

Even more significant than the impact of recycling on national resource deficiencies is the allaying of regional materials shortfalls through recovery from solid waste in densely developed SMSAs such as New York. In an analysis of regional economic growth, the Port Authority (PA) points to a 67 percent gain in manufacturing construction nation-wide in 1973 and contrasts it unfavorably with a 14 percent drop in the New York region, including a 28 percent drop in the New Jersey sector. [10]   A Port Authority proposal for industrial recycling parks traces this to the outmigration from the area of various primary industries. Their absence is blamed for inhibiting the growth of desirable light in-dustries. This is tied to a long-range decline in area-wide manufacturing employment, from 1.9 million jobs in 1953 to 1.5 million in 1971. [11]

According to the PA, this imbalance causes primary materials to be imported into the region at an additional cost to the industries and to the consumer. A review of the 1967 census by the PA reveals that 3.2 million tons of pri-mary metal products were shipped into the area; 2.0 million tons of stone, clay, and glass products; 1.4 million tons of pulp and paper products, and 940,000 tons of fabricated metal products. [12]

This lack of primary processing capacity has also caused the export of 1,246,000 tons of steel scrap through the Port of New York in 1971. Over half of this goes to Japan and Italy, a sizable quantity of which is imported back into the region after being made into steel bars, plates, and tubes. [13] Summarizing, the materials imbalance in the New York region is bad and rapidly becoming worse, a fact which provides a prima facie case for resource recovery.

MARKETING THE PAPER FRACTION

Paper is the foremost target for recovery, comprising approximately one-third of the generated refuse in the study area, or between 15,000 and 20,000 tons per week (TPW) by 1980. Traditionally wastepaper has been used in grades where it did not originate with 40 to 50 percent going to-ward the production of recycled boxboard. [14]   However, both setup and folding boxboard have come into competition with solid bleached sulfate board, a virgin wood product, along with plastics and more flexible packaging. As a result, recycled boxboard capacity has slowed considerably, or, in some cases, virgin fibers are being used at the expense of paper stock to improve appearance. An American Paper Institute (API) compilation of growth trends in paper which includes boxboard and combination corrugated containerboard, shows that recycled paperboard made a meager contribution (0.3 percent per annum) to capacity in the period 1956-74 amid the healthy (6 percent per annum) growth rates of the virgin-based grades (unbleached kraft, solid bleached, and semichemical).[16]

The annual projected gain for the 1975-77 period for recycled paperboard capacity is, however, 3.6 percent. By far the principle contributors to the increase are corrugating medium (43 percent) and linerboard (19 percent). Only modest increases are expected in folding (11 percent), and small to insignificant contributions are expected from container chipboard (15 percent), gypsum board (3 percent), and setup (less than 1 percent).[17]

According to the Midwest Research Institute (MRI) analysis "Paper Recycling: The Art of the Possible 1970-1985," the six paper grades with potential for increased recycling are: (1) corrugating linerboard and (2) corrugating medium, (3) printing/writing paper, (4) tissue paper (5) folding boxboard, and (6) newsprint. Although virgin kraft presently dominates linerboard manufacturing, with recycled fiber use under 10 percent, an MRI study found a new 1,000 tons per day (TPD) mill designed specifically to handle 25 percent secondary fiber would achieve manufacturing costs equivalent to those of a virgin mill, if delivered corrugate could be obtained for $31 per ton.[18] Corrugating medium utilizing waste corrugate presents one of the best prospects for increased recycling.

Overall consumption of waste corrugate for use in the production of medium and linerboard grew by 10.5 percent in 1972, 11.9 percent in 1973, and is projected to grow by 8 to 10 percent through 1975.[19] Weyerhaeuser Company is in the process of establishing several such mills in the United States. One 2100 TPW facility in Raleigh, North Carolina, will derive 30 to 40 percent of its raw material inputs for lineboard and 90 percent of its corrugating medium from old corrugate collected by handpicking or from stores.[20] However, further technological improvements in the manufacturing of recycled medium and linerboard (90 percent plus) are needed if they are to be fully competitive in regards to performance (strength, crush resistance) with semichemical, the virgin grade. This qualitative equivalence is crucial in the establishment of a stable market.

In New Jersey, there are 218 converters of paper and paperboard. They represent a preferred source of waste-paper for the 34 pulping mills.[21] Thirty-six of these are converters of corrugated products which generate corrugated clippings. These represent only an indirect market for waste corrugate. The paper mills which pulp from paper stock (all but four, according to Lockwood's) represent the real market. Since corrugated containerboard mill capacity in New Jersey is already overwhelmingly recycled, the market for increased corrugate recovery appears to lie either in expansion of an existing mill (for which there are no present plans), or the attraction of a new 3,000 TPW facility to the study area. Initially, a contractual agreement with one of the existing mills to take the amount anticipated from handpicking (a potential 831 TPW in 1980; 1,010 in 1985) would be in order. Although the maximum total corrugate recovery projected for 1980 and 1985 (3,010 TPW and 3,704 TPW) could support, and would definitely make desirable, a new facility so as not to glut the market, the decentralized nature of the collection system by private scavengers, local governments, and stores coupled with the fact that some of this is already ging to existing mills, would make this volume uncertain. This contrasts with the establishment of a detinning mill, where the ferrous scrap volume is practically guaranteed. Both of these options need to be investigated by a regional solid waste authority. Additional investigation, determination of volume, coordination, and possibly incentives would be required to attract the mill.

The third grade for increased recycling would be folding boxboard. Since combination boxboard and solid wood pulp board are so distinctly different, no conversion of plants or increased use of secondary inputs is generally possible. MRI found that the only means of replacing the latter with the former is new capacity and that significant pressure would be required to reverse the trend in which an increasing share of production is going to solid wood pulp paperboard. New investment in combination paperboard is discouraged by lack of new demand and the unattractive economic return on capital.[22] In New Jersey all boxboard capacity is recycled and already using close to 100 percent paper stock as inputs. Without incentives, there is little chance of new investment, virgin or recycled, in the state.

The use of old newspapers to make newsprint is the fourth grade for increased recycling. This accounted for only about 18 percent of all old news consumption in 1973, but is a "potentially explosive area for waste paper use in the future."[23] The cost of newsprint manufacture is lowered by using 100 percent recycled fiber, thanks to a new de-inking process. Of the paper grades, newsprint capacity rated the highest projection for the 1975-77 horizon, with an annual expansion rate of 3.4 percent.[24] Even throughout the period of excess wastepaper supply due to economic recession in 1974-75, an urgent need for additional news-print manufacturing capacity was clear. According to Stanford Smith, President of the American Newspaper Publishers Association, Reston, Virginia, an estimated 13 million tons of newsprint will be required in 1980, and there is not in existence or in construction enough manufacturing capacity, including foreign suppliers, to meet that demand.[25] According to the Commerce Department, imported newsprint now represents about 78 percent of United States total news-print consumption, or 8.8 million tons. Garden State Paper Company, which originally started the 100 percent deinked newsprint business in 1961 and is now expanding plants on the west coast, completed in late 1974 an expansion at its Garfield plant, from 150,000 tons per year (TPY) to 215,000 TPY. A new facility must have 300 TPD input of old news or 110,000 TPY to operate profitably, and costs approximately $25 million. Garden State has signed contracts with floor prices with municipalities for news from their curb-side collections, and has been a major force in promoting news collections throughout the state. The company intends to expand wherever and whenever profitable. The study area has a projected quanitity sufficient to support a new mill (2283 TPW in 1980, and 2801 TPW in 1985). However, this assumes a 40 percent recovery by source separation which is too high according to company spokesman John Fedynyshyn, who notes that there are other mills presently competing for the news. The company would have to be convinced there is sufficient obtainable newsprint for any additional expansion in New Jersey.[26] One prospect could be the increased utilization of No. 1 mixed by other mills instead of old news, freeing the waste news for channeling into highly demanded newsprint. If there were to be any expansion in capacity, it would be Garden State, since the company is the only newsprint manufacturer in New Jersey, New York, and Pennsylvania. In any event, the projected handpicked recovered newsprint -- 623 TPW in 1980; 766 TPW in 1985 -- could be marketed with Garden State in a contract agreement.

Printing/writing paper offers one of the greatest potentials for increased recycling, with only 3 percent of

annual production from deinking, and a need for a 50 percent
increase in capacity by 1985.[27] The type of paper stock
needed consists of pulp substituted and high-grade deinking
recovered from paper printing and converting and properly
controlled office waste (register bond, writing paper). The
most promising end uses are groundwood paper, uncoated book
paper, and chemical writing paper. Secondary fiber pulp
from mixed postconsumer wastepaper is not competitive because of low yields and increased waste effluent loads.

The high cost and unavailability of high-grade paper
waste has been the major factor in the demise of wholly
nonvirgin based printing/writing paper producers for the
nation. In New Jersey the industry has not emerged, due to
the economic infeasibility of importing all pulp. However,
the persistence and intensification of a regional pulp
shortage makes a strong case for high-grade wastepaper separation, regardless of the lack of Jersey printing/writing
paper mill capacity. For instance, carefully controlled
office paper recovered by the Port Authority of New York/
New Jersey at the World Trade Center has been marketed as
high-grade deinking waste at upward of $100/per ton.

The establishment of in-state capacity awaits continued developments in deinking technology, which are likely
by 1980. Strength characteristics of the final product are
not the limitation here, as with corrugate container manufacturing, but rather the perfection of the deinking process
to produce a consistently clean, bright paper. Companies
such as Potlatch Corporation are demonstrating at the
pilot plant level (50 TPD) deinking of high-grade postconsumer paper waste for use in their production of printing/
writing and fine papers. A 150-TPD printing/writing paper
mill-based on 50 to 80 percent recycled fiber furnish is
very possible within this 1985 horizon in New Jersey if this
supply of wastepaper can be established. Securing the virgin
balance (30 percent plus) of the furnish would then become
the limiting factor.

Of the 20 percent of other (mixed) paper projected for
recovery by source separation means (2,771 TPW by 1985),
the amount will initially go either into export or No.1
mixed markets for New Jersey mills to make products from
boxboard to insulation paper. Both high grade, postconsumer
deinking and mixed papers have been suggested for over 50
percent of the furnish in the manufacturing of catalog and
directory papers. However, the production of such relatively
low-value products is generally only feasible at obsolete
newsprint mills, where equipment is already fully depreciated.[28]

Wastepaper accounted for 27 percent of production in 1970.[29] There is no technical limit to the amount of waste-paper utilized in tissue production. However, for the most part, due to quality considerations with postconsumer wastepaper, the paper component has primarily been pulp subsitutes and high-grade deinking. The MRI found that usage could be increased by providing postconsumer office paper of guaranteed quality at a price lower than the sources presently in use. Marcal Tissue in West Paterson (80 TPD) is the sole New Jersey mill which could possible utilize carefully sorted office waste. The technology to upgrade mixed paper to a quality suitable for tissue production is presently not available.

A 40 percent overall recovery of wastepaper, as item in the introductory discussion of the projected recovery mix, would supply 26 percent of the fiber consumed in 1985, in contrast with 22.7 percent in 1975.[30] The 26 percent figure may seem disappointing in comparison with the high of 35 percent achieved during World War II. However, the 35 percent rate was during a period of acute pulp shortages, and since that time three-fourths of the nation's pulping capacity, primarily based on forest resources, has been installed.[31]

The United States Forest Service released a report in December 1972 indicating that demand for timber could exceed supply by the early 1980s.[32] MRI's analysis of forest resources indicates that there will be no overall shortage of pulpwood in the time frame considered in 1985, but that regional shortages of pulpwood and increasing pressure on softwoods will amost surely exist, and residue recovery will increase in importance.[33] At that point fiber demand will probably be intense enough to make feasible the recovery of 30 percent of the paper in the waste stream which can be separated by mechanical means. The Black Clawson Fiberclaim process has not yet proved viable due to technological and marketing constraints. The paper is of low quality and is not competitive with source separation of mixed paper.[34] Techniques of upgrading the fiber at a price cost-competitive with fiber sources of higher quality are being investigated by the EPA. Air classification and selective screening are used at a dry separation pilot plant operated by the city of Madison and Forest Products Laboratory. A fraction of paper is obtained which consists of almost entirely newsprint. However, it presently has the same contamination and marketing constraints of wet separation. If pulp fractionation to obtain superior grades of fiber becomes practical, the possibilities are good that increased amounts of wastepaper

EXHIBIT 6.5

WASTEPAPER EXPORTS BY NORTHEAST, 1970-73, NET TONS

Year	Canada	Central America	South America	Italy	Other Europe	Korea	Japan	Taiwan	Other Asia	Total
				IMPORTING COUNTRIES						
1970	2,342	145	4,101	23,969	3,155	1,581	700	216	1,784	37,992
1971	3,418	1,024	4,998	17,418	1,421		1,031	111	2,100	31,521
1972	6,747	332	5,324	14,557	887		604	202	3,950	32,603
1973	3,700	278	7,956	26,146	1,719	11,471	10,223	3,389	5,436	70,318

Source: F. L. Smith, Jr., "Trends in Waste Paper Exports and Their Effects on Domestic Markets," EPA 530 SW-132 (U.S. EPA, 1974), p.4.

can be used in paper-and paperboard-making.[35]   These processes have not been considered as resource recovery options
prior to 1985.

A market of growing importance for both east and west
coasts is the export of wastepaper.   After remaining essentially unchanged for the previous three years, in 1973
wastepaper exports increased 65 percent (268,000 tons).
This increase represented about 20 percent of the total increase in wastepaper recovery.[36]   Although nationwide exports represented 5.1 percent of total paper recovery for
1973, they were heavily west-coast-newsprint oriented, and
represented only 1.6 percent of the total wastepaper recovery in the northeast.   In 1973 the northeast increased
its domestic demand for wastepaper by 180,000 tons, and its
exports by 37,000 tons, for a total increased demand of
217,000 tons.   Northeastern wastepaper use is 32.4 percent
of the national total, and its exports 9.7 percent.[37]
Exhibit 6.5 shows the importing countries of northeast
wastepaper exports.

During the past four years exports to Canada from the
north-central region more than doubled, while exports to
Central America and some Asian countries from the southwest
decreased by over 70 percent.   Korean imports surged and
there were significant increases in imports by Japan and
Taiwan from the west coast, although Asia still received 20
percent of its wastepaper from the northeast.   Exports will
probably grow in importance for the Port of New York area,
but are not yet a major market for the region.

Wastepaper prices result from the interaction of domestic supply and demand with foreign demand.   Paper-converting
industries, of which there are 218 in New Jersey, are sensitive to any changes in disposable income, consumer demand,
and economic downturn, adding to the instability of prices.
The following medium prices (Exhibit 6.6) are regarded to
be reasonable averages for wastepaper prices in normal economic times.   They are not the averages of the extremes
listed.   The Official Board Markets prices refer to prices
at the dealer, which avoids the calculation of a delivery
cost to a mill; MRI estimates appeared in "The Art of the
Possible" (1973).

EXHIBIT 6.6

WASTE PAPER PRICES, 1974
($ per gross ton)

At the Mill (Delivered)		Official Board Markets (Dealer)
Old News		
High 3/74	60	35
Medium (MRI)	27-33	18-22 (MRI)
Garden State	35	15
Low 1/4/75	5-20's	2-5
Corrugate		
High 3/74	65	(35)
Medium: Weyer-		
haeuser	30	(15-20)
Medium (MRI)	--	18-24 (MRI)
Low 1/4/74	5-15	5-10
No. 1 Mixed		
High 3/74	20-25	(15)
Medium	(15-20)	(10)
Medium MRI	--	12-15 (MRI)
Low 1/4/74	5-10	5

Numbers in parentheses are authors' estimates.

For the purposes of the study, a mill price of $25 per ton for newsprint, $30 per ton for corrugate, and $15 per ton of No. 1 mixed has been assumed.

As mentioned at the outset of this chapter, what is needed to stabilize the erratic ups and downs of waste-paper demand and prices is longer-term contract buying between users and suppliers, similar to that of other commodities. In addition, other structural changes which are beyond this study are needed for sizable expansion of paper recycling in New Jersey. A 1972 survey of 82 mills in the New York/Pennsylvania/New Jersey area prepared for the New York City Council on the Environment found that the "New York wastepaper market is already highly developed and will not undergo any significant expansion in the next few years without any massive changes in the nature of the industry."[38] The study also compiled ten factors which mills cited as important in increasing their use of waste-paper.[39]

This section has suggested appropriate channels for the projected wastepaper to be recovered in northern New Jersey. However, the greater national framework must also be kept in mind, as voiced in a <u>Waste Age</u> editorial: "Until and unless we implement some broad based national changes in institutional factors (tax incentives, freight rates), the recycling of paper will continue to be an iffy proposition."[40]

MARKETING THE FERROUS SCRAP

Next to paper and energy recovery, ferrous scrap is the most valuable component of municipal waste. The years 1973 and 1974 were record years for total domestic consumption of scrap, with 102 million and 105.4 million net tons consumed respectively. Whereas production and consumption of home scrap has remained more or less constant around 54 million net tons (N.T.) over the past ten years, purchased domestic (postconsumer) scrap has fluctuated considerably, absorbing most of the 8-million-ton increase in total scrap usage to 1973, and increasing dramatically by 7 million NT to 51.7 million in 1974.[41] In addition, ferrous scrap export in 1973 reached an all-time high of 11.3 million NT in 1970.[42] During 1974 scrap exports were controlled at 2.1 million NT per quarter due to the intense domestic and international demand.

These trends appear encouraging for the increased recovery of steel scrap from waste. However, the recent surges in demand must be viewed in context of the nature of the steel industry itself. Its vertically integrated nature, inertial investment in technologies perfected over the years, and advantages derived from economies of scale of primary industries discourages scrap use even when it is inexpensive. The sharp increase in scrap use has resulted from an unprecedented world demand for steel and foundry products, along with restrictions on the production of pig iron due to coking coal shortages.[43]

The trend which constitutes a more reliable demand for steel scrap is that which represents a change in the nature of steel production: the development of electric arc furnaces, based entirely on scrap charge. This trend is encouraged by growing constraints on iron ore and energy supplies. Iron-ore concessions originally granted to the US Steel and Bethlehem Steel companies to the year 2000 in South American countries have been, or are in the process of being, nationalized.[44] Substantial additional new capacity (15 million to 20 million tons) will be needed to meet anticipated demand for steel in 1980.[45] This increment

will either be met by new electric arc or basic oxygen furnace (BOF) capacity. BOF's which produced more than half
the nation's steel in 1972, can consume only about as much
scrap as the steel mill generates internally (29 percent),
thus eliminating the need for purchased scrap.[46]

Since 1972, however, the growth of electric arc capacity has accelerated, accounting for 27.4 million NT of
steel production in 1973. "Mini-mills," or small electric
arc, continuous casting mills, many underwritten by Japan-
ese or Italian monies, appear to be sprouting up in all
populated parts of the country. Factors favoring their
establishment were enumerated by Jim Brown, director of
Development-Arc Furnaces for the Union Carbide Corporation:
their small size (minimum size requirement 150,000 (gross
tons per year (GTPY); low level of energy consumption
one fourth to one third of a basic steel mill); short installation time; guaranteed regional market and availability of local scrap; rapid return on investment; and
operational flexibility.[47] The development of prereduced
iorn-ore pellets for use in the BOF is the only significant
threat to electric arc dominance of future capacity. In
any event, the utilization of continuous casting by both
big and mini steel will increase the demand for high-grade
obsolete scrap by decreasing the supply of home scrap.

Our projected recovery mixes show an available annual quantity of light ferrous of 131,404 gross tons (2527
times 52) 1980 and 161,720 gross tons for 1985. These
quantities would be less, realistically, unless the waste
from every municipality were processed at either an energy
recovery or resource recovery facility, and would also
appear in increments with successive recovery modules, since
each can efficiently process only 2,000 or 3,000 TPD of
waste. The study area will be generating 8,000 TPD in 1980
and over 9,000 TPD in 1985. The major contaminants in this
fraction would be some aluminum (from bimetal cans) and tin,[48]
both of which are removed by a detinning operation; subsequently the detinned product is marketed as high quality
No. 1 bundle scrap. M & T Chemical, a subsidiary of American Can, which operates several United States detinning
plants (one in Elizabeth at 60,000 GTPY), would pay 35 percent of <u>Iron Age</u> price for No. 1 bundle for the ferrous
metal, according to Jerry Juhasz, marketing manager.[49] The
existing Elizabeth facility could absorb an additional
20,000 GTPY, and a new site handling from 30,000 to over
80,000 would be built proximate to the recovery site if the
ferrous volume was established, according to Juhasz. The
heavy ferrous fraction, 70,980 GTPY in 1980 and 87,308 in
1985, would be marketable directly at the <u>Iron Age</u> price for
No. 2 bundles. Choice of recovery devices for better
marketability and contaminant removal (aluminum and paper),
such as proper hammermill and cleaners before magnetic

separation, should boost the payment received to 40 percent of Iron Age.

Conservative average prices of $32 gross ton (g.t.)
for light and $50 g.t. for heavy ferrous were derived from
an examination of Iron Age prices for the Philadelphia/New
York area over the year and a half prior to writing. These
were then substantiated by estimates of other knowledgeable
sources in the field.

EXHIBIT 6.7

FERROUS SCRAP PRICES, 1974
$ per gross ton

	No.1 Bundle	Light(35%)	Heavy:No.2 Bundle
Low 7/5/73	53.50	18.73	38.83
Medium (average of 2)	89.50	31.33	49.83
High 10/14/74	125.50	44.00	60.83

Source: Iron Age

Juhasz from M & T Chemical estimated a range price for
No. 1 through to 1985 as being $80 to $100 per GT. Steel
industry analyst Dean Peterson stated that prices would continue to fluctuate with the business cycle, but that "we
will never see $60 per GT (for No. 1) again."[50]   More li-
beral estimates were made by the National Center for Resource Recovery, assuming a $40-per GT sale to the detinner
(implicit price of $100 per GT at 40 percent of Iron Age.[51]
The general consensus of M & T, U.S. Steel, and New Jersey
Steel and Structural (NJS&S) representatives was that this
quantity of scrap (both No.1 and No.2) can be marketed without difficulty.

The New York/New Jersey area has a system of scrap brokers with a healthy export market.[52]   Secondly, New Jersey's
only steel mill, New Jersey Steel and Structural, and electric arc continuous casting operation with a raw steel
capacity of 150,000 GTPY, is undertaking expansion to bring
capacity to 300,000 GTPY by 1985. The mini-mill, started up
in July 1973, produces rebars for markets from Boston to
Washington, using a scrap charge of 70 percent No. 1 heavy
melting No.1 bundle and 30 percent shredded steel, secured
from scrap brokers in New York and New Jersey. U.S. Steel
installed in 1973 a new two-electric-arc furnace shop at its
Fairless Works, north of Philadelphia. According to Director
of Public Relations William Peck, the two new furnaces,each
with a scrap charge of 233 tons per heat, comprised of plant
revert, No.1 heavy melting, and No. 1 bundle in varying pro-

portions, are producing 1/2 million tons of basic steel products each year.[53] Since its founding in 1953, nine open
hearth furnaces, producing a total of 4 million TPY from a
charge of 75 percent hot metal, 25 percent scrap have been
installed.

In conclusion, in light of the recent and planned expansion of NJS and S, Fairless, and M & T, it appears the
marketing of the projected amount of scrap would be feasible
for a revenue of $32 per GT and $50 per GT for the light
and heavy fractions, respectively. The establishment of
one 2000-TPD recovery module would produce approximately
30,000 GTPY of light fraction, which would absorb existing
detinning capacity. Further scrap recovery and concurrent
detinning capacity expansion would have to be negotiated
with M & T Chemical officals. The total amount of No. 1
bundle scrap to be generated is actually sufficient to provide the charge for an additional mini-mill.

MARKETING THE GLASS SCRAP

According to our projected recovery mix, approximately
215,176 TPY of glass (4,138 times 52 of crushed glass and
fines) would be available in 1980, increasing to 264,836
TPY by 1985. This quantity would be impacted substantially,
however, by a legislative ban on nonreturnable beverage containers as would the aluminum and steel components. A brief
discussion of this topic is included here because, perhaps
more than aluminum and steel manufacturers, glass manufacturers appear to have more at stake, with their markets being
eroded by plastics and the nonreturnable bottle serving as
the last major growth frontier.[54]

Nonreturnable beverage containers are, foremost, a
litter problem, comprising a minimum of 30 percent of items
collected along roadways.[55] According to Arsen J. Darnay,
deputy assistant administrator for Solid Waste Management
Programs for the EPA, beer and soft-drink containers represent approximately 7 percent of the total institutional, residential, and commercial solid waste.[56] In a report prepared for a group of organizations in the beverage and container industries, Midwest Research Institute found that the
ban would terminate an estimated 66,000 jobs in the steel,
aluminum, metal can, and glass industries; 56,000 jobs
(equivalent of full-time) would be added in beverage production, distribution, and retailing. The jobs lost would far
exceed the skill and pay levels of the jobs gained.[57] According to MRI, the ban would cause an estimated national loss
of about $800 million in tax revenues for the first five
years, as opposed to $210 million for litter collection and

and disposal presently incurred on the state and federal levels.

Regardless of environmental benefits, with the present depressed state of the economy, it is very doubtful that any legislation with unemployment side effects will be considered before 1980. Even at that time, a gradual approach and lead time of several years would be required to allow for the depreciation and replacement of beverage-container capital if major economic disruption were not to be caused.[58] It appears that beverage-container legislation will not be in effect in New Jersey until after 1985, and therefore is not a major concern of this study.[59]

With the returnable-bottle question temporarily shelved in New Jersey, both glass manufacturers and solid waste/resource recovery agencies are being pressured into finding uses for waste glass reclaimed from municipal waste, which would be mixed in color. Color-sorted cullet, mostly internally generated, is presently being used by most glass manufacturers; it saves the plant $2 to $3 per ton of input by producing a faster melt, therefore reduces fuel consumption and refractory wear. Whereas the industry-wide average is about 15 percent of input tonnage, glass quality and high production can be maintained while using cullet levels up to 50 percent. The Glass Container Manufacturer's Institute (GCMI) has adopted 30 percent as a goal.[60] Glass manufactrers will continue to promote their purchasing of consumer segregated glass, which amounts to a very small portion of cullet usage, and possible increase deliberate in-plant cullet production, neither of which will significantly affect the fraction obtainable from municipal waste. Although optically color-sorted cullet has been satisfactorily demonstrated by the EPA-sponsored Black Clawson operation in Franklin, Ohio, the Bureau of Mines, and is to be built into the National Center for Resource Recovery (NCRR) designed full-scale "Recovery I" Facility in New Orleans, color sorting of glass is not proven as cost-effective at this time, although it will be by 1985.[61] So, unlike steel, paper, and aluminium, which utilize existing albeit limited markets, uses for glass salvaged from the waste stream have not yet been established.

There have been, however, significant recent developments in the areas of utilizing a portion of mixed cullet in the production of colored glass, test uses of glasphalt road surfaces, and new building materials containing waste glass. In Dayville, Connecticut, the Glass Container's Corporation has contracted with the Connecticut Resource Recovery Authority to take mixed cullet from a regional solid waste processing facility at a price of $14 per ton delivered.[62] Both the Metro Glass and Brockway Glass plants

in New Jersey make only flint glass. However, Herbert
Snyder, director of Process and Product Development for
Brockway at their headquarters in Brockway, Pennsylvania,
felt there was "no question there would be a market for a
clean, mixed color cullet of this volume on a regular
basis," although he could not say whether it would be with
Brockway or a close competitor.[63] Snyder cited the use of
purchased mixed color glass at the Brockway and Washington,
Pennsylvania, plants, which are 300 miles from the Meadowlands area.

According to Tom Krawiec, promotion director at the
Owens-Illinois plant in Bridgeton, New Jersey, this South
Jersey plant uses a measured combination of brown and green
to produce a specific type of green glass, but no purchased
mixed cullet is currently being employed by a New Jersey
plant.[64] The Owens-Illinois plant in Brockport, New York,
however, purchases mixed cullet,due to difficulties in obtaining cullet and raw material inputs, particularly soda
ash, according to Krawiec. Krawiec predicted that with a
guaranteed supply of mixed cullet, along with increasing
soda-ash shortages, utilization of mixed-color glass in
other Owens-Illinois plants, as in the North Bergen plant
which makes all three colors of glass, was quite probable.
In addition, Krawiec noted that the quantity of mixed glass
anticipated for the study area (4,138 TPW in 1980) would be
more than sufficient to supply one glass furnace a minimum
of 300 TPD, to allow for the test marketing of a new line of
mixed color "ecoglass." In its Industrial Outlook 1975-1980,
the Commerce Department found that soda ash has been, and
will continue to be, in short supply, and that this, along
with energy savings, will increase the demand for cullet.[65]

A promising application for waste glass in northern
New Jersey is as aggregate in bituminous paving. According
to an EPA-sponsored evaluation of 20 glasphalt pavings
undertaken by the University of Missouri, Rolla Civil Engineering Department, performance has been satisfactory in
most instances. These United States and Canadian applications range in intensity from parking lots to industrial
park streets and contain from 25 to 65 percent glass aggregates. Surface degradation was a problem at two locations,
and skid resistance at one. Apparently, glasphalt is less
resistant than conventional pavements to studded tire
damage, despite the attainment of adequate Marshall properties. Ward Malisch and other concluded that glasphalt is
most suitable in less intensive roads because of possibly
low skid resistance.[66]

In May 1972 the Port Authority laid a glasphalt strip
as a cargo service road 200 feet long at Kennedy International Airport. According to Carol Hubert, associate

traffic engineer for the PA's Division of Engineering, the
road strip has been given the ASTM skid resistance test
six times since installation. On November 19, 1973, at
1 year, six months and 1, 150,000 vehicle passes, the
north-bound lane tested 35, and south-bound 40.[67] At the
last reading on September 12, 1974, at 2 year, 4 months
and 1,800,000 vehicle passes, both the north and south
lanes read 30. The friction factor recommended by the
Federal Highway Administration is a minimum of 35.[68] According to Hubert, the PA was not alarmed at the reading,
but would continue to monitor the road. Stuart Millendorf,
director of Environmental Programs for the PA was not dis-
pleased with the road's performance, citing that it had
met standards for over two years. Millendorf felt that
glasphalt has definite possibilities for less intensive road
uses, such as residential roads and parking lots.[69]

In related research, the Midwest Research Institute
found that slurry surfaces containing waste glass provide
effective seals for road bases against moisture penetration,
are skid resistant, and have the advantage of no loose particles of aggregate.[70] The study cites available laboratory data on the resistance to abrasion of cured slurries
containing equal volumes of graded glass (40 percent) and
expanded shale, which show that such mixtures abrade less
rapidly than corresponding mixtures containing only the
best-known crushed-stone aggregate. These same tests indicate that the bond between asphalt and glass is at least
as strong as the bond between asphalt and natural crushed
stone.

It appears that before any wide-scale utilization
of waste glass in paving can be promoted, test data have
to be gathered from whatever sources exist, and several
other experiments, monitored like the PA's testing of the
performance of glasphalt in both intensive and nonintensive
uses, should be undertaken. Appropriate applications
having been determined, the viability of using waste glass
will then be dependent on a resource recovery facility which
can produce the desired gradation and on the installation
of a nearby asphalt plant, which can utilize stockpiled
aggregate with a minimum of handling, as most plants located
in quarries do. Leo Eckmann, district engineer for Asphalt
Institute, East Orange, felt the installation of a plant designed to handle additional waste glass inputs would be
much more feasible than the modification of existing plants.
Some additional natural aggregate would still have to be
brought to the site.

The key to the viability of a glasphalt plant at a resource recovery site would be the state of depletion of natural aggregate in the immediate area. According to Eckmann, the existing quarry in the Meadowlands area will be exhausted before 1985. Additional aggregate is presently being barged down the Hudson from New York State. This seems to suggest a favorable climate for such a facility in the Meadowlands by 1985, market uses having been established by satisfactory test data.

One final application with good prospects is the use of glass as bonding material and building rubble as fill material for making large, fired, ceramic building units. The glass enables low firing temperatures and short firing times, which lead to products with high strength and low water absorption.[72] Three mixtures (13,31, and 94 percent glass) were tested, all with 6 percent clay, the latter mixture showing the highest compressive strength (3.5 times that of high-strength concrete). All three show a greater resistance to rupture than commercial concrete (2 to 5 times) increasing with glass content, and less water absorption. Glass rubble structural panels are seen as competing with large brick panels and precast concrete panels now used in building construction. The facing panels give relatively inexpensive and handsome finishes, with various decorative facings, such as marble and granite.[73] By 1980 demand for wall panels are expected to increase to 1.4 billion square feet (7.5 percent annual growth rate), with the Middle Atlantic, South Atlantic and Pacific states accounting for more than half.[74] The channeling of waste into a new glass wool insulation plant was considered for our study area, but dismissed for the time being, due to the relatively small amount of glass utilized (30 TPD), a market which is not growing rapidly (3 percent annually), and which is dominated by four major firms.[75]

MARKETING THE ALUMINUM AND OTHER NONFERROUS SCRAP

Aluminum is the most valuable commodity on a per-unit per-weight basis in municipal waste, with a value ranging from $200 to $300 per ton. According to aluminum industry sources, 1.6 billion aluminum cans were returned for recycling in 1973, representing about 15 percent of the beverage cans produced in that year. Allowing for 15 percent consumer separation, a maximum of 221 TPW of can stock is anticipated for 1980.

Domestic production of bauxite is expected to remain at about 1.9 million long tons (dried equivalent) per year, with producing states being Arkansas, Alabama, and Georgia.

In the absence of drastic action by major suppliers of United States bauxite, imports will remain at 11 to 12 million long tons, as in 1973.[77]   However, in March 1974 the International Bauxite Association was formed, consisting of Australia, Guinea, Guyana, Jamaica, Sierra Leone, Surinam, and Yugoslavia, for the purposes of achieving higher revenues for bauxite and alumina, and maximum vertical integration of their own industries.   The Commerce Department cites "serious implications" of these actions resulting from extreme dependence on these countries for our imports -- 89 percent of our bauxite and 97 percent of our alumina.[78]   In addition, Jamaica has enacted a Bauxite Production Levy to (at a minimum) quadruple bauxite payments from their 1973 level of approximately $25 million.

Aluminum recovery would be feasible only at a total materials recovery operation.   Methods include gravity separation, magnetic field separation, chemical/thermal, and electrostatic separation.   The first two are the most promising.   The wet sink-float system of separation was developed by Combustion Power Company to process 500 tons per hour of heavy fraction, and improved on by the National Center for Resource Recovery (NCRR), which claimed the earlier recovery rate of 80 percent for aluminum by heavy media separation. This process is currently used by several companies to separate the nonmagnetic fraction of auto shredder scrap.[79] Combustion Power Company pilot plant experience, however, reveals the following technical, economical, and operational uncertainties with the sink-float system: the efficiency of separation of glass and aluminum; waste water treatment; and the large power, facility, and manual control requirements inherent in the system.[80]

As an alternative without these deficiencies, a completely dry separation process featuring a prototype aluminum magnet separator was put into operation at the Combustion Power Company pilot plant in Menlo Park, California in late 1973.   Separation is made by a revolving screen at 5/8 inch, 1 1/2 inches and 4 inches: the minus 5/8 contains most of the glass and stone; the plus 5/8 to minus 1 1/2, the majority of mixed nonaluminum nonferrous; the plus 1 1/2 to minus 4, from 66 percent to 95 percent of the aluminum can stock; and the plus 4 inches is used for reshredding.   The 1 1/2-to-4 inch fraction is fed through an alternating current electromagnetic field where the aluminum can stock is swept laterally off the belt to either side and collected.   The minus-1 1/2 fraction and "trash" from the aluminum separators are fed to nonferrous separator modules, which function as ferro-magnetic pulley-type separators.

The reuse of recycled aluminum can stock by primary producers offers the highest market values of up to $300

per ton. Physical characteristics of the recovered aluminum, including organic residues, amounts of thin sheet and
foil, and particle size will affect the remelt efficiency
and may lower the value to the producer. Because of this,
the Combustion Power Company device has been designed to
recover the can stock primarily, with castings and foil to
a lesser extent so that the product would be within the
limits of Alcoa Grade I can stock. However, concentration
of aluminum can stock in waste varies substantially among
regions, depending on the distribution of all aluminum
beverage containers, and this would have to be determined
for New Jersey. Of three pilot-plant tests, Menlo Park,
St. Louis, and Wilmington, Delaware, can stock recovery
was the greatest at the latter site, where coarse milling
of the refuse was employed. Can stock recovery by the
magnetic separator was 90 percent, and overall can stock
recovery 84 percent.[81]

Nonferrous metals, including aluminum, copper, zinc,
lead, and stainless steel, make up from 1/4 percent to
1 1/2 percent of municipal solid waste, and represent a
value of between $.50 and $4.00 per ton of solid waste.
The market for a mixed nonferrous fraction of copper, brass,
lead, zinc, and stainless is uncertain. Technologies for
further separation have not yet been developed. The two
markets identified by CPC for this mixed nonferrous scrap
quoted values of $200 to $400 per NT. The first full-scale
dry nonferrous recovery system sized to an input solid
waste feed of 50 TPH will be installed at Ames, Iowa, in
1975.

Reynolds Aluminum's eastern region collection center
based in East Rutherford, would be the market for the
study area's recovered aluminum which would subsequently be
shipped after shredding to one of Reynold's primary producing plants in New York of Massachusetts. The revenue to
be assumed in our study is $200 per NT, although the CPC
findings show that given sufficient can distribution for
a sufficient proportion of recoverable can stock, and proper separation techniques, the scrap can be marketed at
$300 per ton, which is the price paid to consumers upon
returning them. Although not currently feasible, an "other
nonferrous" separation module could be added onto the
existing recovery plant in 1985, or whenever the technology
and regional or export demand make it worthwhile.

SUMMARY

Progress toward the goals of instituting a suitable
long-range solid waste disposal strategy for northern
New Jersey and of expanding recycling seem likely in
light of national resource and energy constraints. Utilization of existing markets for waste materials should be
anticipated, but not at the expense of saturation, with
possible displacement of other sources of recyclable material. In particular, we do not want to add to the already ample supply of low quality, marginal, and low-value
secondary material. When at all possible, the emphasis
should be in recovering resources in a way that will produce qualitatively cost-competitive, likely substitutes
for virgin material.

The very nature of our proposal -- its scale, long-
range planning, level of technology, and investment -- will
make it possible to generate new markets. The quality
and quantity of material should enable the construction
of an additional detinning plant, expansion of new or high-
grade deinking capacity, or sufficient waste glass to allow
for the test marketing of new products such as "ecoglass."
Northern New Jersey does not have a large number of growing markets for recoverable materials, although the existing markets are highly developed. It has, however, recently acquired several key facilities, such as Garden
State Paper and New Jersey Steel and Structural, which will
further expand and may attract new capacity to the state.
Most important, northern New Jersey has the density of population to make this degree of recovery possible and to
sustain the development of these types of markets and products.

Recent trends in recycling are encouraging, including
greater separation for higher grades and more direct recycling, and growing cooperation between suppliers and
utilizers of recycled materials by contract agreements.
Both approaches are necessary, for economic survival as
well as for the gradual building of stability into a market which has traditionally been highly erratic. Greater
stability would in turn reduce the strong disincentives
to waste materials use and increased recycling: wide
fluctuations in price, supply, and demand.

NOTES

1. This is in accordance with capital and other cost re-
    quirements estimated in the book.

2. William Franklin, "Paper Recycling: The Art of the
    Possible: 1970-1985" (Kansas City, Mo.: Midwest Re-
    search Institute, 1973), p. 58.

3. Definitions of technical terms:

    Converting: Any process or operation applied to paper
    or paperboard after the normal paper-making operations.
    Converters are industries who process the paper from
    the mill into paper products, by operations such as
    printing, boxmaking, envelope making.

    High Grades: Types of wastepaper which can be sub-
    stituted directly for wood pulp. They are:
        (a) Deinking I: usually bleached papers that have
    gone through a printing operation and are collected
    from printing plants and other converters, and subse-
    quently processed at a deinking mill.
        (b) Pulp substitutes: Clippings and shavings, such
    as envelope and bleached paperboard cuttings, and other
    high-quality fibers derived from paper-converting plants
    and data-processing centers.
    Kraft paper: A paper made predominantly from wood pulp
    produced by a modified sulfate pulping process. It is
    comparatively coarse paper, strong, and in unbleached
    grades is used primarily as a wrapper or packaging ma-
    terial.
    Mixed grade: Covers a wide range of the lowest-quality
    paper stock, consisting of unsorted mixed papers obtain-
    ed from office buildings, printing plants, and other
    commercial. Includes No.1 and No.2 mixed, boxboard cut-
    tings, mill wrappers.
    Residues: The waste of a wood-processing operation, in-
    cluding foresting, primary manufacturing, and lumber-
    board manufacturing. Residues are used for wood pulp
    and other by-products,such as particle board, or are
    disposed of as a waste.
    Semichemical Paperboard: Paperboard made from a furnish
    containing not less than 75 percent virgin wood pulp,
    the predominant portion of which is produced by a semi-
    chemical process.
    Setup boxboard: Paperboard used in making boxes in ri-
    gid form as contrasted with a folding or collapsible
    box; made entirely of wastepaper.
    Softwood: Otherwise known as conifers, they are the
    most common source for paper in the northern hemisphere.
    Sulfate (kraft)pulp: The most important pulp product
    today, it is produced by an alkaline chemical process,

generally utilizing conifers with a high resin content,
such as pine and Douglas fir. It produces the strong-
est fibers, primarily used for paperboard and packaging.
Sulfite pulp: It is an acid pulp used to process low-
resin woods such as spruce, fir, or hemlock, generally
used to make printing grades of paper, and for tissue.

4.   In addition, 100 percent recovery is assumed for over-
tissue news, corrugated clippings, high-grade deinking
I (printing and converting waste), as well as high-grade
pulp substitutes. Since these do not enter the municipal
waste stream, they do not apply here.

5.   The percentage of can stock of total aluminum varies
widely; the percentage in this application was 64 (Wil-
mington, Delaware). Jay A. Campbell, Senior Project
Engineer, "Electromagnetic Separation of Aluminum and
Nonferrous Metals" (Menlo Park, Calif.: Combustion
Power Company, February 24, 1974).

6.   U.S. Department of Commerce, Domestic and International
Business Administration, U.S. Industrial Outlook 1975
with Projections to 1980 (Washington, D.C.: G.P.O. 1974,)
p.7.

7.   Port Authority of New York and New Jersey, Planning and
Development Dept., "The Regional Economy: 1973 Review
and 1974 Outlook" (New York, January 1974), p.10.

8.   Department of Commerce, op.cit., p.8.

9.   National Commission on Materials Policy, Material Needs
and the Environment Today and Tomorrow, final report
(Washington, D.C.: June 1973), p.4 D-8.

10. Port Authority, "The Regional Economy," p.8.

11. Port Authority Planning and Development, "Industrial
Recycling Parks: Opportunities for Regional Economic
Growth," (New York: Port Authority of New York and
New Jersey, June 1973), p. 1.

12. Ibid., p. 15.

13. 678,283 tons went to Japan, 141,643 to Italy, Ibid.,p.
34.

14. S.A. Lingle, Chief Materials Recovery Branch, E.P.A.
"Paper Recycling in the United States," Waste Age, vol.
5, no.8, (November 1974), p. 7.

15. Arsen Darnay and William E. Franklin, "The Role of Packaging in Solid Waste Management 1966 to 1976," SW-5c, (Washington, D.C.: E.P.A., 1969), p.20.

16. American Paper Institute, "Capacity 1973-1976: Paper, Paperboard, Woodpulp with Additional Data for 1977-1979" (New York, 1974), p. 4. Adjusted by cumulative revisions as of February 1, 1975.

17. The balance (approximately 27 percent) is categorized as "other." Calculations derived from API Capacity estimates, "Paperboard by Grade," p. 15.

18. Midwest Research Institute (MRI) "Paper Recycling," p. 85.

19. Lingle, p. 8.

20. Interview, David C. Nicholson, assistant director, Environmental Resources, Weyerhaeuser Company, Tacoma, Washington. Weyerhaeuser currently operates three converting plants in New Jersey (corrugated container/boxboard, corrugated container, and milk carton).

21. Lockwood's Directory of Paper and Allied Trades, 1974 (New York: Lockwood Publishing Company, 1973).

22. MRI, "Paper Recycling," p. 103.

23. Lingle, p. 8.

24. API, p. 4.

25. News Release, New Jersey Committee for Resource Recovery, "Paper Recycling Must Continue, Still Necessary Despite Slump" (Hackensack: Garden State Paper Company, November 1974), p. 6.

26. Procurement Division, Garden State Paper Company, Hackensack, January 1975.

27. MRI, "Paper Recycling", p. 108.

28. Interview with Frank Lorey, corporate technical director, Garden State Paper Company, Garfield, New Jersey April 8, 1975.

29. Ibid., p. 116.

30. MRI, p. 60.

31. *Ibid.*, p. 4.

32. "The Outlook for Timber in the United States," December 1972.

33. MRI, p. 38.

34. Lingle, p. 7.

35. Art Jepson, "Fractionation to Cut Costs, Improve Quality," *Paper Trade Journal*, March 6, 1972.

36. Fred L. Smith, Jr. "Trends in Wastepaper Exports and Their Effects on Domestic Markets," (EPA/530/SW-132), (Washington, D.C.: U.S. EPA, 1974), p. 1.

37. *Ibid.*, Table 6.

38. Gail Shearer, "Four Reports: Markets in Solid Waste," New York City Council on Environment, 1972.

39. Factors ranked were: less contamination, lower wastepaper prices, lower freight rates, more reliable supply, increase in demand for "recycled" products, increase in price stability of paper, high virgin pulp prices, improved technology for upgrading paper stock, decrease in taxes for capital investment made for production equipment for Type I recycled fiber.

40. *Waste Age*, November 1974.

41. AISI estimates, Source: News release, Office of Public Affairs, Cost of Living Council News, Washington, February 15, 1974.

42. *Ibid.* Principle markets for United States scrap are Japan, Taiwan, South Korea, Italy, Spain, Canada, and Mexico.

43. The accompanying prices were compounded by other factors, including critical shortages of railroad gondola cars, scrap-market disruptions created by the CLC, and reduction in the amount of home appliance and automobile scrap available. Bernard Landau, president ISIS, statement in *33 Magazine* (McGraw-Hill publication, July 1974), p. 65.

44. The Venezuelan properties nationalized in January 1975 are Orinoco Mining, a U.S. Steel subsidiary which produced and shipped 85 percent of Venezuela's iron ore to the United States in 1973. From "Venezuela to Pay U.S. Steel Corporation," *Wall Street Journal*, November 29, 1974, p. 4.

45. Department of Commerce, <u>U.S. Industrial Outlook 1975-1980</u>, p. 71.

46. National Commission on Materials Policy "Metal Statistics," 1972, p. 4D-17.

47. <u>33 Magazine</u>, "Mini-Mills," (New York, July 1974).

48. Tinplate, the major tin-mill product used in the production of metal cans, has been losing ground steadily to tin-free steel (TFS) -- a steel sheet coated with a flash of chromium instead of tin. First introduced in the late 1960s, TFS currently represents about 20 percent of tin-mill products used in metal cans, compared with 11 percent in 1969. Tinplated steel is still expected to dominate the can market through 1985. Source: <u>U.S. Industrial Outlook 1975-1980,</u> p. 187.

49. Interview, with J. Juhasz, marketing manager, Rahway office, November 1974.

50. Personal interview, Dean C. Peterson, Materials Division, Commerce Department, November 13, 1974.

51. National Center for Resource Recovery estimate in "Environmental Industrial Park as an Option for Long Range Resource Recovery-- Solid Waste Disposal Planning," unpublished, Washington, August 15, 1974.

52. Although the loss of exported scrap at the same time as ore and concentrates are imported is regrettable, exports will provide a boost and a buffer to fluctuations in the domestic market until a more solid domestic demand via new E. Arc. capacity develops.

53. Peck could not be definite about any expansion at Fairless by 1985, but stated that continuous expansion was a company goal. Interview, November 1974.

54. Arsen Darnay and William E. Franklin, "The Role of Packaging in Solid Waste Management 1966 to 1975," SW-5c (Washington, D.C.: E.P.A., 1969).

55. Tayler H. Bingham and Paul F. Mulligan, Research Triangle Institute, "The Beverage Container Problem," EPA-R2-72-059 (Washington, D.C.: E.P.A. Office of Research and Monitoring, 1972.)

56. Arsen Darnay, testimony, regarding Beverage Container legislation before the New York State Council of Environmental Advisors, February 20, 1974.

57. Jeff Maillie, "The National Economic Impact of a Ban on Nonrefillable Beverage Containers," final report (Midwest Research Institute, June 30, 1971, executive summary).

58. Testimony of Darnay.

59. Hearings on Deposit Bottle legislation were held in Trenton in November 1974, according to Mike Catania, legislative research, with no results.

60. Arsen Darnay and William E. Franklin, "Salvage Markets for Materials in Solid Waste 1966 to 1976," (Washington, D.C.: EPA, 1972), p. 70.

61. Source: Harvey Gerschman, NCRR, November 1974, and "Recovery I" promotional pamphlet, also NCRR.

62. Ibid.

63. Interview, January 2, 1975.

64. Interview, January 2, 1975.

65. Pp. 182-183.

66. Ward R. Malisch, Delbert E. Day, and Bobby G. Wixson, "Use of Domestic Waste Glass For Urban Paving," University of Missouri, E.P.A. Office of Research and Monitoring, Contract No. USPHS RO1 - EPO 329, February 1973.

67. Conversations in December 1974 with Carol Hubert, traffic engineering, Division of Engineering, Port Authority of New York and New Jersey.

68. Readings have fluctuated up and down, according to Ms. Hubert. The ASTM skid resistance test is measured with a type 300 trailer riding @ 40 mph over a wet pavement with one bald tire locked for a few seconds in a panic stop. Of course many roads do not meet these standards.

69. Interview, December 1974.

70. Midwest Research Institute, "The Commercial Potential of Slurry Seal with Waste Glass Aggregate" (Washington, D.C.: Glass Container Manufacturers Institute, 1971), p. 7.

71. Conversations with Leo Eckmann, December 1974 and January 1975.

72. T. C. Schutt, H. Campbell, and J. H. Abrahams, "Build-
     ing Materials Containing Waste Glass," American Ceramic
     Society Bulletin, vol. 51, no. 9 (1972), pp. 670-671.

73. Such a glass-rubble plant would require (in 1972 dollars)
     a total capital investment of $6 million ($3 million
     fixed, 1.4 million amortized, and 1.7 million recover-
     able). Midwest Research Institute, "The Commercial
     Potential of Glass-Rubble Building Panels" (Washington,
     D.C.: Glass Container Manufacturers Institute, 1971).

74. Ibid., p. 22.

75. Information from the Midwest Research Institute report,
     "The Commercial Potential of Glass Wood Insulation"
     (Washington, D.C.: Glass Container Manufacturers
     Institute, 1971).

76. U.S. Industrial Outlook 1975-1980, p. 188.

77. Major countries of origin are Jamaica, Surinam, Do-
     minican Republic, Guinea, Guyana, Haiti, and Australia.
     Ibid., p. 73.

78. Ibid., p. 74.

79. To separate aluminum, which has a specific gravity of
     2.6 to 2.8, from other metals, which have specific
     gravities greater than 2.8, a medium of intermediate
     density is used. In such a situation, aluminum parti-
     cles would float while all other nonferrous particles
     would sink. Source: "Recovery of Aluminum from Solid
     Waste" Resource Recovery, reprinted from January/
     February/March issues, 1974.

80. Jay A. Campbell, "Electromagnetic Separation of
     Aluminium and Nonferrous Metals,"(Menlo Park, Calif.
     Combustion Power Company, Inc., February 24, 1974).

81. Ibid., p. 15.

CHAPTER 7

TECHNOLOGICAL ALTERNATIVES

This chapter reviews the major technological alternatives: (1) incineration, (2) dry fuel, (3) pyrolysis, (4) the recycling park, and (5) landfilling. The four nonlandfilling choices are considered in order of increasing complexity. Incineration has the longest operating record; the recycling park is a new concept.

INCINERATION

Incineration is a proven technology. Unfortunately, politics and economics led us to rule it out as a choice for northern New Jersey. Our review of the technology will therefore be brief.

Incinerators burn refuse in an excess oxygen atmosphere in order to achieve an 80 to 85 percent volume and 60 to 65 percent weight reduction. The incineration system has six major components: (1) a receiving and storage area; (2) a technology to move the solid waste into the furnace; (3) a furnace to fire the waste; (4) fans and other equipment required to deliver oxygen into the furnace; (5) a stack and emissions control system; and (6) methods of removing noncombustible residues.

The two important technology choices are refractory and waterwall. The walls and ceilings of refractory units are lined with materials which possess refracting properties. In order to protect the structure while maintaining an acceptable throughput, excess air must be pumped into the furnace to remove the heat. The excess air carries off

particulates as well as heat. The results are air emissions
which have all but ended the usefulness of the refractory
technology.

The refractory system has given way to the waterwall
technology. The furnace walls consist of vertical metal
tubes joined by metal fins. Radiant energy produced by incineration passes through the fins and tubes and converts water
in the tubes to steam. Fossil fuels can be used to superheat
the steam for electric generation. By passing the radiant
energy through the fins and tubes, the system can operate
at high temperatures and the amount of air needed is far less
than for the refractory technology. Air quality problems are
greatly reduced and revenues can be obtained for the steam.

Three recent attempts to build incinerators in the study
area were rejected and so led us to conclude that the technology is not politically acceptable for our planning period.[2]
First, the lower Passaic Valley Solid Waste Management Authority
(Quad City) sought to construct an incinerator to serve the
communities of Paterson, Clifton, Passaic, and Wayne. Second,
Joint Meeting Number One tried to develop an incinerator to
serve seven Essex County municipalities. Third, the Hackensack Meadowlands Development Commission's attempt to build
the world's largest incinerator -- 6,000 plus TPD -- at a cost
of $125 million was rejected. Economic and environmental fac-
tors entered into the decision. Frankly, however, the citizens
of the region do not want to be near a facility which in the
past was considered to be at best an eyesore.

Economics also argues against incineration. Landfilling
in the Meadowlands always has been much cheaper than incineration alternatives. And at the present time, both dry fuel
and pyrolysis appear to be less costly systems than incineration. A comparison of incineration with steam recovery, incineration with electric generation, dry fuel, and gas pyrolysis
costs suggests that at medium revenue credits, dry fuel and
pyrolysis have a $3 - to $5 - per-ton advantage over incineration.[3]

REFUSE/FUEL RECOVERY SYSTEMS

A major type of energy recovery that may be developed in
the northern New Jersey area involves the use of processed
dry refuse as a supplemental fuel in electric power production.
This approach was first applied in a joint venture between
the city of St. Louis, Missouri, and the Union Electric Company, and partially supported by the U.S. Environmental

Protection Agency. Municipal solid waste collected by the
city is shredded and separated into light combustible and
heavy noncombustible fractions by air classification. The
light combustibles are then transported to the utility's
electric generating station where they are fired pneumati-
cally into existing boilers as a supplemental fuel along
with pulverized coal. Approximately 10 percent of the
energy requirements of these boilers are provided by this
refuse fuel.[4]

Magnetic metals are recovered from the heavy fraction
and the remaining metals, glass ceramics, and other heavy residues are landfilled. These processes use equipment already commercially available. The St. Louis system is designed to handle 325 tons of refuse per eight-hour day with
a maximum daily throughput of 650 tons for a two-shift operation. This demonstration project has been in routine but
intermittent operation since April 1972 and has operated
as predicted.[5]

As a result of this successful demonstration project,
the Union Electric Company will invest $70 million over the
next five years to construct a regional system of refuse
processing and transfer facilities to convert approximately
8,000 tons per day of municipal refuse into fuel for use
in its generating station in the St. Louis area. The system
will be owned and operated by a subsidiary of Union Electirc
as a private business. The estimated disposal cost of this
regional system will be competitive with landfilling in the
region.[6] Similar regional-scale applications of the dry
fuel recovery system are also underway in the state of
Connecticut where five facilities, designed to process
7,000 to 10,000 tons of refuse per day are under construction
or planned for operation before 1980;[7] and in the seven
state Tenessee Valley Authority region, where six plants
processing 7,400 tons of refuse daily are planned for operation during the next three to five years.[8]

During the past two years, the success of the St. Louis
project and the independent research and development efforts
of other public and private agencies have prompted the development of dry fuel recovery facilities in many areas of
the country. Approximately fifteen to twenty such projects
are now planned or under construction with a combined processing capacity of 19,000 to 20,000 tons of refuse per day.
All of these facilities are expected to be fully operational
by 1980.[9] The smallest dry fuel processing plant recently
began operations in Ames, Iowa, where 200 tons of municipal
refuse per day will be converted into fuel for use in a
municipal power plant.[10]

Dry fuel recovery has also been investigated for possible use in the New York - New Jersey metropolitan region. A study of eight solid waste management proposals prepared for the Hackensack Meadowlands Development Commission (HMDC) concluded that the dry fuel recovery process most nearly satisfies the solid waste management and resource recovery objectives of the Meadowlands district.[11] The HMDC recently committed itself to the development of large-scale resource recovery facilities in the Meadowlands before 1980, Although alternative recovery systems are also under study by the HMDC, the dry fuel recovery process remains the preferred technology.[12]

New York City and Consolidated Edison Company also completed a study of combining 6,200 tons of refuse fuel with oil in eight utility boilers in the city. The estimated capital cost of this system is $70 million for processing and transportation facilities, and $15 million for fuel receiving and firing facilities and boiler modifications at three of the utilities generating stations.[13] The estimated net disposal cost of this system would be $8.28 per ton of refuse assuming a fuel credit to the city based on the prevailing price of No. 6 fuel oil, which in 1973 was $4.50 per barrel.[14] Depending on present system costs, major increases in the price of fuel oil since 1973 could substantially reduce the cost of this system to levels competitive with landfilling. Dry fueld recovery systems have also been studied for potential application in Essex, Middlesex, and Union Counties in New Jersey.

Overall, this system must be considered a leading candidate for early development in the northern New Jersey region because of the successful performance of the St. Louis demonstration project, subsequent developments in other areas of the country, and the high level of interest centering on the dry fuel recovery system in the New York-New Jersey metropolitan region.

Unit operations involved in the preparation of supplemental fuel from refuse are: (1) refuse receiving and primary shredding; (2) air-gravity spearation of the refuse stream into generally light organic and heavy inorganic substreams; (3) the secondary shredding of the organic portion to produce the final fuel product; (4) the magnetic separation of ferrous metals from the heavy inorganic material; and (5) the further classification, separation, and cleaning of the nonferrous metals and glass in the residue, which may be added as recovery processes and product economics permit. A typical process is described below and illustrated in Exhibit 7.1.[15]

Incoming municipal refuse is weighed and dumped into a receiving pit equipped with a live bottom conveyor system. As the refuse moves from the pit, clean wastepaper and card-

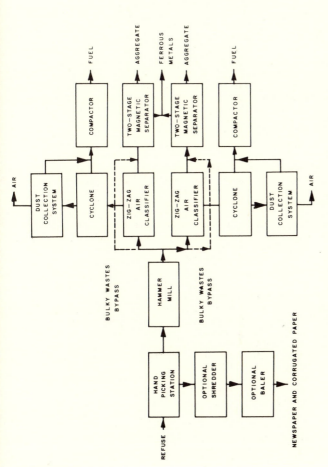

EXHIBIT 7.1 Dry—Fuel Recovery Process

board are handpicked and conveyed either directly to the
baler or to a shredder which reduces the size to a maximum
of 8 inches. The baler compresses the paper and cardboard
to approximately 50 pounds-per-cubic-foot bundles, 30 inches square by 6 feet in length. Approximately 5 to 10
percent of the refuse could be reclaimed by handpicking of
cardboard and newspapers.

The remaining raw refuse is fed to a horizontal shaft
hammermill shredder by a short vibrating feeder. The hammermill shreds the refuse down to the 2 - 4 - inch-particle-
size range. The shredded refuse is conveyed to two zigzag
air classifiers where the refuse is forced to follow a
zigzag path which loosens the refuse, knocking out grit and
other debris trapped in the feed. The light fraction of
the refuse (i.e., papers, plastics, organic matter, etc.)
is pulled upward in the air column while the heavier fraction
tumbles downward, releasing any entrained light material as
it falls. The heavy fraction consists predominantly of
ferrous and nonferrous metals, glass, wood, rocks, and heavy
plastics. This primary separation helps to reduce the contamination of the ferrous metal fraction in the magnetic
separator. The twin air classification system provides a
50 percent alternate capacity in the event of a mechanical
failure in either air classification system.

The light fraction (paper and plastics) from the top of
the zigzag air classifier is blown into the cyclone separators where the light fraction is separated from the air
stream. In the cyclone separator most of the light fraction
falls to the bottom and the carrier air containing dust flows
into the dust collection system before being vented to the
atmosphere. Both the material from the primary cyclone and
the dust collector are compacted for sale as a boiler fuel.

The heavy fraction from the bottom of the air classifiers is conveyed to a magnetic separator where the ferrous
metals are removed. The nonmagnetic material consists of
glass, aluminum, wood, heavy plastic, rubber and dirt. Aluminum is handpicked from the nonmagnetic fraction and the
rest of the fraction is sent to landfill. The ferrous metals,
essentially tin cans, are then ready for detinning at either
on-site or off-site facilities. In the detinning process, a
high quality ferrous scrap is produced as well as tin. A
bypass system can also be incorporated for use when handling
special materials that need not be air classified; for example, white goods, on special collection days.

This system can be developed in modular processing lines
to provide redundancy and total capacities ranging from 500
to 2,500 tons per day.

The end products of this particular process are:

Boiler fuel	60%
Ferrous Metals	7%
Aluminum	5%
Paper (newsprint & corrugated)	8%
Moisture loss	10%
Residue	15%

Total 100% by weight

The marketability of the material products is described in Chapter 6. The following discussion centers on the potential markets for the dry fuel product, particularly its use as a supplemental fuel in electric power generation. It should be noted, however, that this fuel also has a potential market for use in large industrial power plants and in certain industrial processes such as cement making.

Most of the processing steps previously described are designed to improve the energy value and handling qualities of the refuse fuel product. This is achieved by reducing its moisture content, separating out noncombustible materials such as metals and glass, and by reducing and standardizing the particles of refuse fuel to levels that permit relatively easy handling and rapid and complete combustion.

As a result, the refuse fuel product has an energy value of 5,000 to 6,000 BTUs per pound, or approximately 40 to 50 percent of coal. Its moisture content is typically 10 percent or less, which retards decomposition, prevents odors, and permits relatively long-term storage of one to two weeks. Its homogenized physical form allows routine handling, storage, and transportation by methods presently available in industry. Refuse fuel has a sulfur content below that of coal or oil although its ash content is considerably higher.

In most applications now under development, solid waste fuel will replace 10 to 15 percent of the heat energy derived from burning coal, oil, or gas in electric generating plants. Experience in St. Louis and elsewhere indicates that a fuel replacement rate of 20 percent can also be considered realistic for most power plants. It also appears that solid waste derived fuel can be used economically in almost any boiler that has bottom ash handling and air pollution control equipment. This includes tangentially fired, front-fired, opposed-fired, cyclone-fired, and stoker-fired units of conventional design. Also included are boilers currently burning gas or oil, although boiler manufacturers conservatively recommend an initial fuel replacement rate of no more than 10 percent with fuel oil. However, even at this modest rate the potential application of refuse-derived fuel in electric power plants in northern New Jersey would produce a number of significant economic and energy-related benefits.

A recent study prepared for the U.S. Environmental Protection Agency surveyed the availability and capacity of utility boilers with the potential ability of using processed solid waste as a supplemental fuel. This study included public and investor-owned power plants in 28 states using data provided by the Federal Power Commission and by the utilities themselves.[17] A study of large industrial boilers is also underway. For New Jersey, the study found that if the state's 2.96 million tons of municipal solid waste could be used as a source of supplemental fuel in electric power generation, it could supply 9 to 10 percent of the state's total electric power requirement in 1971.[18] This represents a potential fuel oil savings of 4.3 million barrels per year. At present fuel oil prices (approximately $13.40 per barrel) this would represent an economic savings to the state's utility companies of $57.5 million per year. By 1980 anticipated increase in both conventional fuel oil prices and the quantity of solid waste derived fuels could produce even larger energy and economic savings for the state.

Because the northern New Jersey region contains the bulk of the state's electric power generating capacity and solid waste production, most of these energy and economic benefits would occur there. Approximately 11 percent of this region's electric power requirements could be met by using processed refuse as a fuel supplement in electric generating stations in this area. This would produce a savings in conventional fuel oil of about 3.7 million barrels per year, an amount equal to 23 percent of this region's total fuel oil consumption for residential, commercial, and industrial purposes in 1971.[19] Put differently, the large-scale use of refuse-derived fuels in electric power generation could produce a substantial increase in the quantity of fuel oil available for other purposes in northern New Jersey without increasing the level of oil imports or redirecting refining capacities away from other valuable fuel products such as gasoline and jet fuel. The potential economic savings to the region would be approximately $49 million per year at present fuel oil prices. Exhibit 7.2 contains a listing of the major electric power generating stations in northern

EXHIBIT 7.2

ESTIMATED REFUSE COMBUSTION CAPACITY OF SELECTED ELECTRIC POWER PLANTS
1971

Generating Station	*Refuse Combustion Capacity*	
	Tons Per Day	Tons Per Week [a]
Bergen	1,180	5,900
Hudson	1,915	9,575
Marion	270	1,350
Kearny	610	3,050
Essex	725	3,625
Linden	1,540	7,700
Sewaren [b]	1,910	9,550
Total	8,150	40,750
1980 Solid Waste Production [c]	10,600	52,995
Refuse Fuel Potential [d]	6,360	31,800
1985 Solid Waste Production [c]	11,993	59,964
Refuse Fuel Potential [d]	7,195	35,978

[a]Five days per week.
[b]Located in northern Middlesex County.
[c]See Chapter 5.
[d]Assumes an average recovery efficiency of 60% for dry fuel recovery
systems.

Source: Where the Boilers Are (Washington, D.C.: U.S. Environmental
Protection Agency, 1974), pp. 183-186, 190.

New Jersey together with their potential refuse combustion capacity. For comparative purposes, the region's estimated solid waste production and refuse-derived fuel potential for 1980 and 1985 are also included. All of these generating stations are owned by Public Service Electric and Gas Company.

At this exhibit indicates, northern New Jersey's seven major generating stations have the present potential capacity to utilize this region's total refuse fuel production through 1985, assuming that they can all accept at least 10 percent of their fuel requirement from processed solid waste and that 60 percent of the region's municipal refuse can be recovered for this purpose. With slight increases in their average consumption rate, these existing facilities could probably provide adequate "disposal" capacity for refuse-derived fuels until 1990 or later.

It should be noted, however, that the foregoing discussion by itself does not indicate that Public Service Electric and Gas Company (PSE&G) or any utility will, or even can, burn prepared refuse fuel in its boilers. There are a number of technical and economic factors which are different for each utility power plant and producing region that determine their respective ability or willingness to use refuse fuel in electric power generation. Some of these key factors pertinent to the northern New Jersey region are discussed below.

The use of refuse fuel in oil-fired boilers has not been tested in full-scale operations. To date, refuse fuel has always been burned together with coal in electric utility boilers. Although a number of research and development projects are underway in various regions of the country, the results of these efforts may not be available for two or three years. Since nearly all electric generating stations in northern New Jersey are oil-fired, the absence of performance data on the use of refuse fuel with oil may prevent the early development of this recovery process in the study area.

Facilities for receiving, storing, and firing refuse fuel will have to be constructed at each generating station, and individual boilers will have to be modified to some degree to accept this new fuel. The capital cost of developing these facilities and of modifying utility boilers in the study area are presently unknown but could be substantial. And because these facilities and improvements would be on utility property, their cost would have to be borne by the utility itself.

The factors affecting the total amount of these investments would depend on the number, age, and type of boilers to be used, the type of normal fuel, the method of firing, and the configuration of the refuse firing system. Additional factors include the present means of ash handling and air pollution control, interest rates and public utility regulations.

Recent estimates prepared for New York City and Consolidated Edison Company suggest that it may cost between $1.7 and $2.6 million to convert each of the 25 boilers in the northern New Jersey area into refuse fuel ready for burning.[20] The estimated total capital cost to the utility might therefore range between $42.5 and $65 million. The selection of individual boilers and generating stations to be included in the system may also be determined by the amount of capital investments required.

Only the Union Electric Company in St. Louis, Missouri, has made investments of this magnitude in order to use refuse-derived fuel. As previously noted, Union Electric's decision to build a $70 million regional fuel recovery system occurred only after five years of active research and development. For dry fuel recovery to be fully successful in northern New Jersey, Public Service Electric and Gas Company will have to become an active and committed financial partner in such a venture.

The utility will also incur some additional operating costs for using refuse fuel in its boilers. These costs might range from $3 to $5 per ton or about $5 million to $8 million per year in addition to the cost of the refuse fuel. These costs would include the amortization of necessary capital investments, additional costs of handling the refuse fuel, associated maintenance of fuel handling and firing systems and boilers, and ash handling and air pollution control costs above normal levels. These costs would have to be developed and monitored for individual boilers and generating stations. Particularly high-cost applications may have to be eliminated.

The actual feasibility of modifying all utility boilers in the study area to accept refuse fuel is unknown. Although there is a growing likelihood that most of these boilers, like similar boilers elsewhere, can be modified to accept refuse fuel, the actual number, location, and capacity of these boilers is not presently known. Physical or operational problems may prevent the use of some boilers or entire generating plants. Conversely some generating stations may be able to accept more than 10 percent of their energy require-

ments from refuse fuel. Such changes would undoubtedly affect the overall capacity, costs, and transportation and
siting patterns of entire systems.

Although the results from the St. Louis project are
encouraging, the long-term effects of using refuse fuel on
the efficiency and reliability of utility boilers is unknown.
Utility companies in the New York-New Jersey metropolitan
area share a common objective and problem in maintaining
adequate and reliable electric generating capacity to meet
this region's large and growing demand. As a result, a great
deal of concern and activity is directed toward preventing
service interruptions, frequent or prolonged downtime and increased maintenance costs. As a result, utilities and their
regulatory agencies may be extremely reluctant to expose
base-load electric utility boilers to any additional risks
of this type that might result from burning refuse fuel.

Although refuse fuel is low in sulfur, its high ash content and the presence of other potentially polluting elements
such as chlorine, require that its use be carefully monitored
and controlled. The northern New Jersey region is already
considered a stressed environment with respect to air and
water pollution problems. The use of refuse fuel to solve
the region's solid waste problem should not aggravate these
already serious problems.

Potential air pollution problems may be avoided, however, due to the limited use of refuse fuel as a supplemental (10 to 20 percent) energy source. Air quality tests
performed at the Union Electric facility in St. Louis indicate that particulate emissions increase slightly when solid
waste is burned with coal, and that gaseous emissions of
sulfur oxides, nitrogen oxides, hydrogen chloride, and mer-
cury vapor are not significantly affected.[21]

The future planned introduction of nuclear generating
facilities in the PSE & G system will cause the load factor
of the fossil fuel plants to be reduced, thereby reducing
the amount of refuse fuel they can accept. Some older, in-
efficient fossil fuel plants may also be taken off line as
base-load power generators as a result of this shift toward
a nuclear base. It appears, however, that this shift may
not occur as rapidly as planned for reasons inherent in the
planning, siting, and developing of nuclear power plants
near populated areas. As a result, this region may continue
to rely heavily on its fossil fuel power plants for the
forseeable future. However, any major changes in the operating characteristics or the planned closing of any existing
facilities will have an effect on the economics and operations of the region's dry fuel recovery system. These potential effects must be identified and accommodated within any
solid waste management/energy recovery plan.

The estimated capital and operating costs of the dry
fuel recovery system are presented below in two parts: (1)
those costs associated with the refuse fuel processing facility and (2) those related to the use of the fuel product
by the utility. As previously indicated, it is assumed
that all costs associated with the construction and operation of processing facilities would be borne by a public
agency or authority that would receive its revenue from user
fees and from the sale of fuel and material products. The
utility would pay those capital and operating costs involved
in receiving, storing, and firing the refuse fuel, together
with necessary boiler modification and air and water pollution control. It is further assumed that as a fuel commodity,
refuse fuel would be sold to the utility at a price commen-
surate with its energy value and the costs of its production
and end use.

Estimated capital and operating costs for refuse fuel
processing facilities have been prepared to reflect present
construction and operating costs in northern New Jersey.[22]
These cost estimates are presented in Exhibit 7.3 for selected facility capacities. The estimated capital cost for this
type of facility ranges from $7.3 million for a capacity of
500 tons per day to $25 million for 2,500 tons per day.
Four or five of the largest (over 2,000 tons per day) of
these plants would be needed to provide northern New Jersey
with adequate solid waste disposal capacity in 1980. Therefore, the estimated total capital costs for this regional
system would be approximately $100 million. Gross operating
costs before credits for recovered fuel and material products
range from $11.09 to $7.28 per ton of refuse input, depending on facility size.

As previously noted, the estimated capital costs incurred by the utility are highly speculative at this time.
However, an average cost of $42.5 million has been suggested
by the study team for the modification of boilers and the
construction of refuse fuel receiving, storing, and firing
facilities at each of PSE & G's seven generating stations in
the study area. The amortized cost of these investments
together with the operating costs to be borne by the utility
are equally uncertain, depending as they do on the capital
investment required, interest rates, and operating conditions
of each facility. For the purposes of this analysis it was
assumed that the utility's average annual operating costs,
including amortization, would be $4.53 per ton of refuse
fuel. This is approximately 50 percent greater than similar
estimates for using refuse fuel in nine utility boilers
owned by Consolidated Edison Company in New York City.[23] It
is also generally consistent with estimates from other sources.[24]

EXHIBIT 7.3

ESTIMATED CAPITAL AND OPERATING COSTS DRY FUEL RECOVERY PROCESS
LATE 1974

	Capacity (Tons Per Day)			
	500	1,000	2,000	2,500
Capital Cost ($000)	$7,300	$11,828	$19,200	$25,000
Annual Cost ($000)	$1,665	$ 2,702	$ 4,385	$ 5,460
Unit Cost ($ Per Ton)	$ 11.09	$ 9.01	$ 7.31	$ 7.28

It is assumed that the price paid by the utility for the refuse fuel would be discounted by this amount to produce
realistic estimates of overall system costs.

The potential value of processed municipal refuse as a
utility boiler fuel depends on its energy value (BTUs per
pound or ton) and on the prevailing price of alternative
fuels, in this case No. 6 residual fuel oil. Although higher
estimates have been offered, this analysis assumes that the
average energy value of the refuse fuel product is 6,000
BTUs per pound or 10 million per ton.

Due to the dramatic increase in the price of fuel oil
in recent years, three alternative price levels for No.6 oil
were used in this analysis. The first or low price level
used is $4.95 per barrel ($0.79 per million BTUs) which
corresponds to the actual delivered price of No. 6 fuel oil
in January 1973. A "high" level of $13.39 per barrel ($2.14
per million BTUs) was used to approximate current fuel oil
prices. This price corresponds to the actual delivered price
of No. 6 oil in May 1974.[25] The simple average of these
high and low prices was used to produce a "medium" price
of $9.17 per barrel ($1.47 per million BTUs). This latter
price was used consistently throughout the study to produce
reasonably conservative estimates of refuse fuel value.
Exhibit 7.4 contains a summary of the estimated net value
of the refuse fuel at these selected price levels.

In applying the dry fuel recovery system to northern
New Jersey, it was assumed that, at least in its early
stages, the only other product recovered for sale would be
ferrous metals, which would produce a net revenue after
transportation and handling costs of $1.08 per ton of refuse
input. This price is also conservative in comparison with
other estimates. Exhibit 7.5 presents the net cost of the
dry fuel recovery system at selected operating capacities
after credits for the recovered fuel and ferrous metal products.

It should be noted from this last exhibit that, at the
lowest fuel price level, net operating costs of the two
largest facilities approach the present cost of landfilling
in the northern New Jersey region. At the medium price level
all operating capacities produce net costs below present landfill prices. At this level the largest facilities produce
a negative operating cost (net revenues or cost savings) of
over $1.60 per ton. At the high price level, which approxi-
mates present prices for No.6 fuel oil, all operating scales
produce negative operating costs ranging from $2.68 to $6.49
per ton of refuse input.

EXHIBIT 7.4

ESTIMATED PRODUCT VALUE OF REFUSE FUEL AND REFUSE INPUT
AT SELECTED PRICE LEVELS

	No.6 Fuel Oil[a] *($ per barrel)*	*Refuse Fuel* *Gross Value*[b] *($ per ton)*	*Net Value*[c] *($ per ton)*	*Refuse Input*[d] *($ per ton)*
Low	$ 4.95	$ 9.48	$ 4.95	$ 2.97
Medium	9.17	17.64	13.11	7.83
High	13.39	25.68	21.15	12.69

[a]The low base price of $4.95 per barrel ($0.79 per million BTUs) was the actual delivered price of No. 6 fuel oil, F.O.B. New York Barges, in January 1973. The high base price of $13.39 per barrel ($2.14 per million BTUs) was the actual delivered price of No. 6 oil, F.O.B. New York Barges in May 1974. The medium base price of $9.17 per barrel ($1.47 per million BTUs) is the simple average of high and low prices. The high an low base price levels are from the Oil and Gas Journal, January 1973 and June 1974, respectively.

[b]Assumes an average energy value of 12 million BTUs per ton (6,000 BTUs per pound).

[c]Includes a discount of $4.53 per ton to the utility for capital and operating costs incurred in using refuse fuel.

[d]Assumes an average refuse fuel recovery rate of 60% of total refuse input by weight.

EXHIBIT 7.5

ESTIMATED NET COST OF DRY FUEL RECOVERY SYSTEM AT SELECTED
CAPACITIES AND PRICE LEVELS
($ per ton of refuse)

| Price Level | | *Processing Capacity (tons per day)* | | | |
		500	1000	2000	2500
Low	Operating Cost[a]	$11.09	$ 9.01	$ 7.31	$ 7.28
	Net Product Credits [b]	4.05	4.05	4.05	4.05
	Net Cost	$ 7.04	$ 4.96	$ 3.26	$ 3.23
Medium	Operating Cost	$11.09	$ 9.01	$ 7.31	$ 7.28
	Net Product Credits	8.91	8.91	8.91	8.91
	Net Cost [c]	$ 2.18	$ .10	- $ 1.60	- $ 1.63
	Operating Cost	$11.09	$ 9.01	$ 7.31	$ 7.28
	Net Product Credits	13.77	13.77	13.77	13.77
	Net Cost	-$ 2.68	-$ 4.76	- $ 6.46	- $ 6.49

[a]See Exhibit 7.3 for summary of estimated capital and operating costs.

[b]See Exhibit 7.4 for net refuse fuel credits at selected price levels. Also includes a credit of $1.08 per ton of refuse for recovered ferrous metals.

[c]Negative net operating costs indicates that net product revenues exceed operating costs. However, these net costs do not include the cost of transporting the refuse fuel to market or the costs of residue transportation and disposal.

These net costs or revenues do not include the cost of transporting the refuse fuel from the processing plant to the utility or the transportation and disposal costs for the process residue. These additional costs would be of particular significance for a regional system employing facilities with lower operating levels, since this assumes a larger number of facilities and longer overall hauling distances. Although a discount to the utility of $4.53 per ton of refuse fuel is included, this amount could vary substantially for each generating station receiving the refuse fuel and produce higher or lower net product values.

While the system's analysis model employed in this study does account for fuel transportation and residue transportation and disposal costs, it can only predict the impact of changes in the utility discount by iteration. It appears, however, that at the high product price level considerable changes in the utility discount would produce only modest changes in net operating costs.

The previous discussion suggests that the recovery of refuse fuel from municipal solid waste for use as a utility boiler fuel would have a number of significant advantages in northern New Jersey. Some of the most important of these are:

1. Technological simplicity and flexibility. Experience in St. Louis and elsewhere indicates that a consistently high quality fuel product can be produced through a combination of relatively simple and reliable mechanical processes already in industrial use or under active development. The quality and quantity of the fuel product can also be adjusted by the addition of slightly different or redundant processing stages, such as secondary shredding or air classifying and screening without difficulty or major added expense. Material recovery systems for nonferrous metals and glass can also be added without affecting the fuel recovery process (although they may increase the energy value of the fuel product by separating out additional contaminants and noncombustible material).

2. The energy recovery potential of this system approaches 80 percent of the energy value contained in municipal refuse.

3. The capital cost of the dry fuel recovery system appears to be less than one-half the cost of

thermal processing systems at comparable
scales. The estimated capital cost of a
2,000-ton-per-day incinerator with electric
power generation is $47.6 million. The es-
timated cost of a dry fuel recovery facility at
this scale is $19.2 million.

4.   At present fuel price levels, the net operat-
      ing cost of fuel recovery systems is compet-
      itive or potentially lower than the cost of
      conventional landfilling in northern New Jersey.
      The average price of commercial landfilling in
      the study area ranges from $2.70 to $3 per ton.
      As previously noted, net processing costs for
      large-scale (2,000 tons per day) fuel recovery
      facilities range from a high of $3.26 to a low
      of -$6.46 per ton of refuse input.

5.   The use of refuse fuel as a fuel supplement in
      electric power generation could displace 10
      to 20 percent of the conventional fuels used
      by electric utilities in northern New Jersey.
      The large-scale use of refuse fuel for this
      purpose could produce a 20 to 25 percent in-
      crease in the quantity of fuel oil available
      for other uses and generate a savings to the
      region and its utilities of $40 to 50 million
      per year in fuel import costs.

The major limitation of this recovery system concerns
the ability and willingness of electric utilities to use
refuse fuel as a supplemental energy source in electric
power generation. More detailed study is needed to determine the capital and operating limits, as well as the air
pollution implications of using refuse fuel for this purpose.

THE PYROLYSIS ALTERNATIVES

The third major group of resource recovery technologies considered for use in the northern New Jersey area is
pyrolysis. Pyrolysis is the physical and chemical decomposition of organic matter brought about by the application
of heat (1,000 to 3,000 degrees F°) in the absence of oxygen
or in a controlled oxygen environment. Unlike combustion
processes, which produce primarily heat and carbon dioxide,
the pyrolysis of organic material involves the distillation
of this material into three component streams: (1) a gas
consisting primarily of hydrogen, methane, carbon monoxide,
and carbon dioxide; (2) a tar or oil that is liquid at room
temperature and includes organic chemicals such as acetic

acid, acetane and methonal; and (3) a char consisting of almost pure carbon together with any inorganic materials such as glass, metal, or rock which may pass through the system. The exact composition and relative quantities of these various streams depend primarily on the composition of the refuse input, pyrolysis temperature and pressure, and the length of time the refuse remains in the pyrolysis reactor.

In recent years, the application of pyrolysis technology to urban solid waste disposal has been the focus of increased interest and research by both public and private agencies. The principal reasons for this increased effort are the ability of most pyrolysis systems to reduce substantially the volume of refuse requiring disposal to a greater degree and in a manner less environmentally hazardous than conventional incineration. The second major benefit, common to most pyrolysis systems, is the ability to convert the organic portion of the refuse into a usable energy product. The type and value of this energy depends on the operating characteristics of the particular system.

Approximately ten to twelve different pyrolysis systems are in various stages of development at the present time. Three of these systems are now being developed and tested for commercial operation and could be available for large-use scale in the northern New Jersey region by 1980: the Monsanto Landgard low-temperature system now under construction in Baltimore, Maryland, to provide steam for district heating in the downtown area of the city; the Garrett Research and Development Company's "flash" pyrolysis system under development in San Diego, California, to produce an oil-like liquid product for sale as a boiler fuel; and the high-temperature Purox system developed by Union Carbide, Inc., which produces a gaseous product that may be used as a boiler fuel or as a chemical feedstock.

Pyrolysis with Steam Recovery

Monsanto is presently completing construction of a 1,000-ton-per-day low-temperature pyrolysis facility in Baltimore, Maryland. When this system becomes fully operational later this year, it will produce 200,000 pounds per hour of low-temperature steam to be sold to the Baltimore Gas and Electric Company for use in district heating in downtown Baltimore. Ferrous metals and a glassy aggregate will also be recovered from the residue. The aggregate will be used by the city in road paving. A carbon char equal to

15 to 25 percent by weight of the refuse input is also produced as residue and will be landfilled.[26]

This facility is being built on a five-acre industrial
site one mile from the city's central business district. A
schematic diagram of this pyrolysis process is shown in
Exhibit 7.6. Unit operations include refuse receiving and
storage, shredding and secondary storage, pyrolysis of shredded refuse, gas purification, steam generation, gas scrub-
bing, residue quenching, and magnetic metals recovery.

Incoming mixed municipal solid waste is shredded to
produce a uniform particle size and to equalize the moisture
content of the refuse. It is then stored in an enclosed bin
having a capacity of 2,000 tons. This secondary storage unit
together with an additional 2,000-ton storage capacity in the
receiving area minimizes interruptions by minor downstream
delays and allows the pyrolysis process to continue 24 hours
per day, seven days per week.[27]

The shredded refuse is fed into a single, rotating refractory-lined kiln or pyrolyzer at the rate of approximately
42 tons per hour. In this unit the refuse is partially burned
in an oxygen-deficient atmosphere to decompose organic matter
into gaseous products, carbon char, metals, and ash. Complete pyrolysis is achieved by burning additional fuel oil
in the kiln at the rate of 8 gallons per ton of refuse.[28]

The solid residue of this process passes through a water
quench and a magnetic separator for removal of iron and steel.
The carbon char is removed from the residue by a flotation
process, leaving the glassy aggregate as the final product.

The pyrolysis gases are burned in a refractory-lined
combustion chamber or purifier to increase their temperature
to 2,000 degrees F. Waste heat boilers are then employed to
recover approximately 200,000 pounds of steam per hour.
The final products of this combustion process pass through a
wet scrubber to eliminate particulates and a reheater to
reduce the steam plume. Waste water is partially treated
on-site and then discharged into the sanitary sewer system.
A 4500-foot pipe line transports the steam product to the
downtown area.[29] All process water is recycled through the
system. Excess waste water will be discharged into the city's
sanitary sewer system to receive treatment. The facility has
had an air quality emission problem but is guaranteed
by the company. The carbon char must be disposed of in a
sanitary landfill to prevent water-soluble materials 11 percent by weight from plluting the ground water.[30]

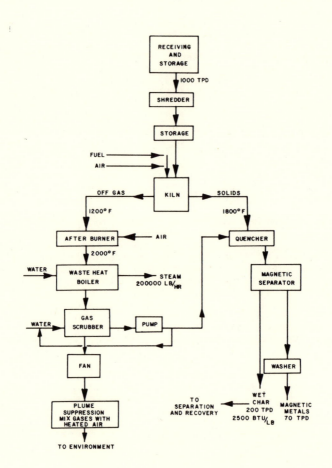

EXHIBIT 7.6   Monsanto Landgard System

The estimated cost of this facility is $16 to $20 million, including land, off-site developments, and construction overhead. The cost of this demonstration project is being shared by the city of Baltimore, the Maryland Environmental Services Authority, and the U.S. Environmental Protection Agency. Upon completion of successful operating   tests, ownership of the facility will be transferred to the city under a "turn-key" agreement with the developer. For this transfer to take place the facility must meet all existing federal, state, and local air pollution regulations, operate continuously at an average of 85 percent of design capacity for a 60-day period and maintain the putrescible content of the residue below 0.2 percent. A performance penalty of up to $4 million may be collected by the city if the facility fails to meet any of these requirements.[31]

The estimated gross unit cost of this system is $7.60 per ton of refuse input. Under the terms of the five-year marketing agreement with the utility, the price the city will receive for the steam product is a function of the prevailing price of No. 6 fuel oil the utility would use to produce the steam. As a result of recent dramatic increases in the price of conventional fuel oil, the net cost of this system after credit for the sale of the steam, ferrous metals, and the glassy aggregate is estimated to be $0.02 per ton.

This type of system has a potential application in electric power generation and may also be constructed at larger operating scales, although specific economic and operational data are not presently available for these variations. Overall, present estimates indicate that this pyrolysis system at 1,000 TPD has substantially lower capital and operating costs than waterwall incineration and net operating costs below existing sanitary landfills of similar size.

Since no market presently exists in northern New Jersey for steam for district heating and specific market opportunities for industrial process use of this steam could not be identified, this recovery system was excluded from further study.   However, it remains a potentially feasible technology if adequate industrial steam markets can be found.

Oil Pyrolysis

On a smaller scale, the Garrett Research and Development Company, a subsidiary of Occidental Petroleum Company, is constructing a 200-ton-per day pyrolysis facility in San Diego, California, designed to produce a low-sulfur oil-like liquid with a heating value (on a volumetric·basis) of 60 to 70 percent of residual fuel oil. This pyrolysis "oil" can

be substituted for or blended with conventional heavy fuel
oil for use in electric power generation or in large industrial power plants.[32] Due to its unique and complex chemical properties, this synthetic oil cannot be refined into
other fuel or chemical products.

When fully operational in late 1976, this pilot facility will produce approximately one barrel of pyrolysis
oil per ton of organic refuse input.[33] Ferrous metals and a
sand-sized mixed-color glass cullet 99 percent plus pure
will also be recovered from this process. The pyrolysis
oil from the Garrett facility will be sold to the San Diego
Gas and Electric Company for use in electric power generation.[34]

A schematic diagram of the Garrett oil pyrolysis process
is shown in Exhibit 7.7. Unit operations in this system include refuse receiving and storage, primary shredding and
air classification to remove inorganic materials, drying,
screening and fine shredding of organic materials, pyrolysis
of the fine shredded material, char removal, gas condensation
and liquid recover. Outlet gases and wastewater are partially treated and a portion of each is returned to the system
for cooling or further processing.

This is the most complex of the three pyrolysis systems
considered here and the one with the most critical performance requirements. Nearly all inorganic materials must be
removed, and the organic portion must be reduced to small
dry particles. As a result, incoming municipal refuse is
shredded to a particle size of 2 inches or less and then
separated into the light organic fraction and the heavier
inorganic portion. The inorganic fraction is then dried
to a moisture content of 3 percent, screened to remove additional inorganics and finely shredded prior to the pyrolysis
process. Ferrous metals are magnetically reclaimed from the
heavy fraction and the fine mixed-color glass cutlet is recovered by selective crushing and screening, followed by
froth flotation.[35]

The pyrolysis reaction itself produces a gas which is
cooled and condensed into the oil product, a char which is
partially reused as fuel in the reactor, and water, a portion
of which is used for cooling purposes. This system produces
solid, liquid, and gaseous effluents requiring additional
treatment and/or disposal by other means.[36]

The synthetic "oil" produced by this pyrolysis process
is a complex oxygen-rich organic fluid that can be substi-
tued for or blended with residual fuel oil. Some typical

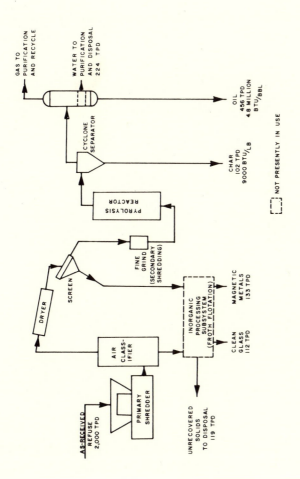

EXHIBIT 7.7   Garrett Research and Development Corporation

EXHIBIT 7.8

TYPICAL PROPERTIES OF NO. 6 FUEL OIL AND PYROLYTIC OIL

	No. 6	*Pyrolytic Oil*
Sulfur (% by weight)	0.5 - 3.5	0.1 - 0.3
Chlorine (% by weight)	--	0.3
Ash (% by weight)	0.5	0.2 - 0.4
Nitrogen (% by weight)	2.0	0.9
Oxygen		33.4
Heating Value (BTU per pound)	18,200	10,500
Volumetric Heating Value (BTU per barrel)	6.2 mm per BBL	4.78 mm per BBL
Pumping Temperature (F)	115	160
Atomization Temperature (F)	220	240

Source: C.S. Finney and D. Garrett "The Flash Pyrolysis of Solid Waste," Presented at Annual Meeting, American Institute of Chemical Engineering, Philadelphia, November 11, 1973, p.186.

properties of these two fuels are compared in Exhibit 7.8.
As this exhibit indicates, the sulfur content of pyrolysis
oil is substantially lower than even high quality residual
oils. However, nearly twice the weight of this product is
needed to obtain the same amount of energy as No.6 fuel.
However, fuel oils are generally sold on a volume basis
(gallon or barrel) and, when compared on this basis, it can
be seen that pyrolysis oil contains about 76 percent of the
heat energy available in residual fuel oil.

Pilot laboratory tests indicate that pyrolysis oil can
be blended with No. 6 fuel oil and successfully burned in
utility boilers with properly designed fuels handling and
firing systems. Negligible amounts of unburned carbon or
other potential pollutants result from this burning process.
Although pyrolysis oil tends to separate after extended
periods of storage and to be mildly acidic, blending this
fuel with No. 6 oil may effectively counteract both of these
problems.[37]

The potential application of this type of energy recovery system in northern New Jersey led us to develop separate capital and operating cost estimates for oil pyrolysis systems at varying operating levels and at selected
price levels for residual fuel oil in the New York/New Jersey
metropolitan area. Capital and operating cost estimates
were derived from earlier national average cost estimates
prepared by the Midwest Research Institute for 1971. The
adjusted cost estimates for northern New Jersey in 1974 are
shown in Exhibit 7.9. Net revenues for recovered fuel,
metal, and glass products at selected price levels are
shown in Exhibit 7.10, together with their respective impacts
on net operating costs.

EXHIBIT 7.9

OIL PYROLYSIS SYSTEM
Estimated Capital & Operating Costs
at Selected Capacities 1974 [a]

| | | | CAPACITY | |
	250 TPD	*500 TPD*	*1000 TPD*	*2000 TPD*
Capital Cost ($000)	$6,509	$11,192	$19,250	$35,093
Operating Cost ($ per ton)	$23.12	$19.89	$17.10	$14.70

Updated to 1974 for northern New Jersey by the study team
from national average estimates prepared by the Midwest Research Institute, in <u>Resource Recovery, The State of Technology,</u> prepared for the Council on Environmental Quality,
February 1973, pp. 38 and 39.

EXHIBIT 7.10

OIL PYROLYSIS SYSTEM
ESTIMATED NET REVENUES AND NET OPERATING COSTS 1974

			CAPACITY		
		500 TPD	*500 TPD*	*1000 TPD*	*2000 TPD*
1.	Annual Operating Costs ($ Per Ton)	$23.12	$19.98	$17.10	$14.70
2.	Net Revenues ($ Per ton of refuse)				
	Medium [a]	7.33	7.33	7.33	7.33
	High [b]	9.86	9.86	9.86	9.86
3.	Net Operating Costs ($ Per Ton)				
	Medium	15.79	12.56	9.77	7.37
	High	13.26	10.03	7.24	4.84

[a]Net revenues at this level assume an average price of residual fuel oil
(No.6) to be $9.17 per barrel with approximately 60%, or $5.50 per barrel, being received for pyrolysis "oil" after deductions for its lower
energy value and for transportation and handling. Therefore, a net credit of $5.50 per ton of refuse would result, assuming a net recovery
and sale of one barrel of pyrolysis oil per ton of refuse. Additional
products credits of $1.08 and $.75 per ton of refuse for ferrous metals
and mixed glass cullet are assumed.

[b]Net revenues at this level assume an average price of $13.39 per barrel
for residual fuel oil, with 60 percent, or $8.03 per barrel, being re-
ceived for pyrolysis oil. All other revenue credits remain as noted
above.

As Exhibit 7.10 and the previous system description suggest, the oil pyrolysis process is the most complex of the pyrolysis systems considered. This complexity and the relatively large number of processing steps are reflected in substantially higher annual operating costs than for either the steam or gas recovery pyrolysis systems. Even with a high average revenue for recovered products, oil pyrolysis is more expensive than either of these other systems. This system does have a lower capital and net operating cost than waterwall incineration with electric power generation at all operating and revenue levels. However, it would be more expensive than new sanitary landfills at current fuel prices.

As the development of oil pyrolysis systems proceeds, additional and more reliable capital and operating cost data will become available. Similarly, the marketability and economic value of the pyrolysis "oil" will become clearer, making more rigorous economic analysis possible. Although this type of energy recovery system should remain a potentially feasible alternative for northern New Jersey, it was not included in this analysis for the reasons noted above.

High Temperature Gas Pyrolysis

The high temperature gas pyrolysis system being developed by Union Carbide appears to have a number of advantages of particular value to the northern New Jersey region:

1.   It does not produce solid, gaseous, or liquid effluents requiring sophisticated or expensive control measures or treatment. System outputs consist of a marketable gas product and an inert slag suitable for use as clean fill. As a result, system complexity and operating costs are reduced and environmental pollution is avoided.[38]

2.   The clean gas product produced by this system is more versatile than steam or synthetic oil. This fuel gas which has a heating value of 300 BTU per cubic foot can be substituted for higher quality natural gas (1,000 BTUs per cubic foot) in existing utility boilers to produce electricity or in large industrial boilers to produce steam for process use or for heating and cooling. This gas may also be used as a feedstock in certain chemical processes to produce methanol and other chemical products. Alternatively, it can be used to generate electric power on-site in standard gas turbine generators.[39]

3.   The solid residue produced by this system is less than 3 percent of the original volume of refuse. This biologically inert material appears to be suitable for use as clean fill, for certain construction purposes, and for road

construction. If suitable markets for this residue can be
developed, volume reduction and resource recovery would
approach 100 percent of the refuse input.[40]

    4.   "Front-end" recovery systems for the reclamation
of ferrous and nonferrous metals and glass can be added
to this system without measurable effects on its operating
characteristics or fuel output. In response to all of these
potential benefits, Public Service Electric and Gas Company
and the Middlesex County Solid Waste Management program are
actively evaluating the near-term application of gas pyrolysis systems in northern and central New Jersey. This energy
recovery system has also been studied for New York City and
Westchester County, New York.

    The most fully developed example of this type of pyroly-
sis system has been constructed by the Linde Division of
Union Carbide, in South Charleston, West Virginia. This
200 TPD demonstration facility has been operated regularly
although intermittently during the past year to gain operating experience and to test the following alternatives:
(1) the direct use of unprocessed municipal refuse; (2) the
addition of shredding and ferrous metals recovery; and (3)
the addition of selected quantities of sewage sludge to the
refuse input. Evaluation of the first two operating modes
has recently been completed with positive results. The
third and final alternative will be tested early in 1976.[41]

    The following description refers to the first and simple-
est operating mode that was selected for use in this study.
Exhibit 7.11 contains a schematic diagram of the Union Carbide system. The key element in this process is a vertical
shaft furnace. Solid waste is fed into the top of the furnace
through an interlocking feeder. Oxygen, at the rate of 0.2
ton per ton of solid waste, is blown into the base of the
solid waste column, where it reacts with char, the solid residue remaining after the pyrolysis of the solid waste. The
resultant combustion is at a high enough temperature (3000
degrees F.) to melt all noncombustible materials in the
residue. This molten metal and glass drains continuously
into a water quench tank where it forms a hard, granular
material.[42]

    The hot gases formed by the reaction of the oxygen and
char rise up through the descending solid waste, providing
the heat needed to pyrolyze the solid waste. No external
fuel supply is needed to drive the pyrolysis reaction. In
the upper portion of the furnace, the gas is cooled further
as it dries the incoming solid waste. This lowers the temperature of the gas exhausting from the furnace to about

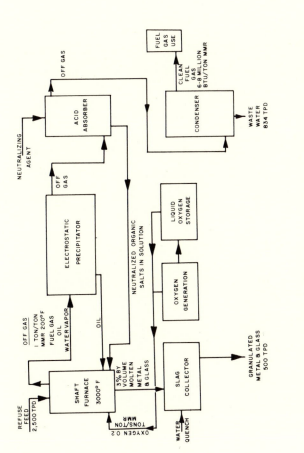

EXHIBIT 7.11 Linde Oxygen Refuse Converter (Union Carbide Purox System)

200 degrees F. The exhaust gas contains considerable water vapor, some oil mist, and minor amounts of particulates and other undesirable constitutents. These components are removed in a gas cleaning train consisting of an electrostatic precipitator, an acid absorption column, and a condenser.[43]

This process has an energy recovery efficiency of 70 to 75 percent by recovering approximately 5.75 million BTUs per ton of refuse. The fuel gas resulting from the pyrolysis process is a clean-burning fuel comparable to natural gas in combustion characteristics, but with a heating value of about 300 BTUs per cubic foot. It is essentially free of sulfur compounds and nitrogen oxides. This fuel burns at approximately the same temperatu as natural gas. The volume of combustion air needed pe₁ illion BTUs is about 80 percent of that needed for natural gas. These characteristics are so close to natural gas that it should be possible to substitute this gas for natural gas in an existing facility. The only plant modification would entail enlarging the burner nozzle because a larger volume of gas must be introduced into the furnace in order to obtain the same heat input.[44]

The limitation on the use of this gas is the extra cost of compressing it for storage and shipment. Because of its low energy value power, consumption per million BTUs to compress it will be 3.1 times greater than for natural gas. As a result, markets for this gas should not be more than one or two miles from the producing facility and only short-term storage should be contemplated. It should be noted, however, that the solid waste plan for Westchester County indicated that pyrolysis gas can be feasibly transported by pipeline from a facility located at Croton Point across the Hudson River to the Consolidated Edison Company electric generating station at Bowline Point in Rockland County, a distance of approximately four miles.[45]

The basic gas pyrolysis process described above may also be combined with on-site gas turbine generators to produce electric power for sale. The pyrolysis facility would need only to be near an electric utility transmission line or substation or a large industrial power user to find a suitable market. Exhibit 7.12 contains estimates of the electric power potentially marketable by combining the gas pyrolysis process with conventional gas turbine generators at selected operating capacities.

The feasibility of this last variation will depend on the ability of the gas pyrolysis/turbine system to provide continuous base-load electric power to meet both market and and waste disposal requirements,the opportunity cost of sell-

the gas product itself, and the market price for the electric power.

EXHIBIT 7.12

MARKETABLE ELECTRIC POWER FROM GAS PYROLYSIS SYSTEMS WITH ON-SITE GAS TURBINE GENERATORS

Operating Capacity (Tons per day)	Marketable Power[a] (KW)
1,000 [b]	21,100
1,500	31,670
2,000	42,200
3,000	63,300

[a]Marketable power excludes electric power produced on-site but consumed for self-support purposes. This self-support requirement ranges from 7,000 to 21,000 KW, depending on operating capacity.

[b]Estimates for the 1,000 TPD operating capacity were interpolated by the project team from Schulz, pp.41,45, and 47.

Base load electric power in northern New Jersey presently has a lower value than peak-load power typically produced by gas turbines. The higher value for peak-load power reflects the relative inefficiency of gas turbines in contrast to very large steam-powered generating plants and the relatively high capital and operating cost of gas turbines being charged off against their intermittent use. The high temperatures and pressure associated with gas turbine operations may also affect their ability to provide continuous base-load power generation.

Estimated capital and operating costs for large-scale gas pyrolysis systems in the New York/New Jersey metropolitan area have recently been developed by the Columbia School of Engineering and Applied Science. These estimates are for gas pyrolysis systems operating at 2,000 and 3,000 tons per day respectively. From these estimates and other sources, the study team also developed capital and operating cost estimates for this system at 1,000 to 3,000 tons per day. The estimates are presented in Exhibit 7.13.

Cost estimates are also available for gas pyrolysis systems with on-site electric power generation at operating capacities of 750 tons, 1,000 tons, 1,500 tons, and 3,000 tons per day, respectively. More detailed consideration of the potential use of the gas pyrolysis/power generation systems in northern New Jersey will be given in future follow-up studies.

The estimated net cost of the basic gas pyrolysis system at selected operating capacities is presented in Exhibit 7.14 together with the respective annual costs and estimated product revenues at low, medium, and high price levels. In this analysis it was assumed that marketable products from this system would be limited to the fuel gas for use as a boiler fuel in electric power generation and the sterile residue for use in road base construction. No credit is given here for recovered ferrous metals.

The price of the fuel gas product is assumed to be equal to the prevailing price of natural gas to electric utilities. Because of potential for substantial near-term increases in the price of natural gas as utility fuel, three price levels were included in this analysis: a low price of $.75 per mm BTU, which is comparable to the present price of natural gas; a high price of $1.75 per million BTU; and a medium price of $1.25 per mm BTU, or the simple average of the low and high prices. The estimated price and revenue for the sterile residue is assumed to remain constant at $2 per ton or $.50 per ton of refuse input.

A review of Exhibit 7.14 indicates the following:

1. At present fuel gas prices gas pyrolysis becomes competitive with new sanitary landfills only at the 3000-ton-per-day operating level.

2. At medium gas price levels both 2,000 - and 3,000 - ton-per-day facilities are competitive with both new and existing landfills in the study area.

3. At the high product price level, pyrolysis facilities at all operating capacities are competitive with present and future landfills. At this price level, product revenues appear to offset operating costs producing modest net revenues of $.07 and $1.12 at 2,000 TPD and 3,000 TPD , respectively.

Overall, the gas pyrolysis system could produce a number of significant economic benefits for the northern New Jersey region and should therefore be considered a leading candidate for early development as part of this region's solid waste management system. Some of the principal benefits of this system are:

EXHIBIT 7.13

GAS PYROLYSIS SYSTEM ESTIMATED CAPITAL REQUIREMENT
AND OPERATING COSTS 1974

	Operating Capacity (tons per day)		
	1,000	*2,000*	*3,000*
Capital Requirements ($000)			
Pyrolysis System [a]	$15,000	$26,116	$36,123
Self-Support Power [b] System	4,150	7,232	9,284
Pipeline & Gas Com-[c] pressor	8,350	8,402	8,823
Total Capital Require- ments	$27,500	$41,750	$54,230
Operating Costs ($000 per year)			
Labor [d]	$ 810	$ 1,206	$ 1,746
Power & Utilities [e]	47	95	142
Maintenance & Supplies[f]	555	839	1,151
Business & Adminis- tration [g]	28	41	58
Amortization of Plant [h]	2,450	3,685	5,056
Amortization of Pipeline[i]	660	660	660
Total Annual Costs			
$000 per year	4,550	6,526	8,813
$ per ton	$ 14.58	$ 10.53	$ 9.48

[a]Includes the cost of the pyrolysis furnace, refuse feed system, gas cleaning system, slag conveyor, and oxygen plant.

[b]Includes the cost of on-site gas turbine generators to provide all necessary power to support the pyrolysis process, oxygen production, and all other subsidiary functions.

[c]Includes the construction of a 36 inch diameter pipeline for a maximum distance of four miles at an average cost of $400 per linear foot. The cost of fuel gas compressors is also included.

[d]Estimated average cost of salaries, wages, and fringe benefits for 45, 67, and 97 employees, respectively, is $18,000 per person.

[e]Provides for supplemental power, sewer and water, and other utility services.

(continued)

EXHIBIT 7.13 (continued)

GAS PYROLYSIS SYSTEM ESTIMATED CAPITAL REQUIREMENT
AND OPERATING COSTS 1974

---

[f]25% of total capital requirements.

[g]2% of the sum of total capital requirements plus maintenance and supply.
requirements.

[h]Assumes an interest rate of 7% for 15 years on all plant facilities.

[i]Assumes an interest rate of 7% for 30 years on the gas fuel pipeline.

EXHIBIT 7.14

GAS PYROLYSIS SYSTEM ESTIMATED PRODUCT REVENUES AND NET COST

	Processing Capacity (tons per day)		
	1,000	*2,000*	*3,000*
1. Annual Operating Cost [a] ($ per ton)	$14.58	$10.53	$9.48
2. Product Revenues [b] ($ per ton)			
Low	4.83	4.83	4.83
Medium	7.71	7.71	7.71
High	10.60	10.60	10.60
3. Estimated Net Cost ($ per ton)			
Low	9.75	5.70	4.67
Medium	6.87	2.82	1.79
High	3.98	.07	-1.12

[a]From Exhibit 7.13.

[b]The following estimated fuel gas credits were used in this
analysis: lo - $.75 per mm BTU; medium - $1.25 per mm BTU;
medium - $1.25 per mm BTU; high - $1.75 per mm BTU for approximately 5.75 mm BTUs per ton of refuse input. The value
of the sterile residue for road construction purposes was
assumed to remain constant at $2 per ton or $.50 per ton of
refuse input.

1.   Simplicity and flexibility of operating modes.
      Additional front-end materials recovery compo-
      nents and back-end electric power generation can
      be added without adversely affecting the basic
      gas pyrolysis process.

2.   A relatively high (70 to 75 percent) energy re-
      covery efficiency and large (95 to 100 percent)
      volume reduction capability.

3.   The absence of gaseous, liquid, or solid effluents
      requiring further treatment or disposal.

4.   The ability to produce a clean and versatile
      fuel product that can be substituted for natural
      gas in electric power generation without major
      system changes or as a feed stock in certain
      petro-chemical processes.

The important disadvantages of the gas pyrolysis system
include:

1.   Very large capital requirements.

2.   The need to be relatively close to fuel gas mar-
      kets may limit locational choices and affect over-
      all system costs.

3.   Large-scale operations require region-wide plan-
      ning and management.

4.   System economics and operating experience is based
      on demonstration-scale facilities.

To test the feasibility of the gas pyrolysis technology
within the context of northern New Jersey's overall solid
waste management system, the study team included this process in its analysis model with the following choices and
assumptions:

1.   Recovered products will consist of fuel gas to be
      sold as boiler fuel in electric power generation
      and inert slag for use in road construction.
      Future analysis will include ferrous metals re-
      covery and on-site electric power generation.

2.   Because of the need to be near fuel gas markets,
      the efficiency of pyrolysis facilities will be
      tested adjacent to the Bergen, Kearny, Essex and
      Linden generating stations. Since the capacity
      of these generating stations to consume fuel gas
      far exceeds the potential quantity available

from pyrolysis processes, the number and location of processing facilities were selected by the study team to provide adequate and relatively convenient refuse disposal capacity throughout the study area.

3. The operating capacities for each gas pyrolysis facility in 1980 will be as follows:

    Kearny: 3,000 tons per day;

    Newark: 3,000 tons per day;

    Linden: 2,000 tons per day;

    Bergen: 2,000 tons per day.

4. The cost of transporting the fuel gas from the processing plants to the generating stations has been included in the estimated capital and operating costs of each processing facility; therefore, no secondary transportation costs or links are necessary in this application.

5. The inert slag produced by this system will be sold for road construction purposes, producing at net revenue of $.50 per ton of refuse input F.O.B. the processing plant. Therefore, no secondary transportation and disposal costs are included in this analysis.

In Chapter 8, three product price levels are tested in consecutive computer runs to determine the overall cost of building, operating, and bringing waste to dry fuel and gas pyrolysis energy recovery facilities. The implications of changing product prices on the size and location of the facilities are stressed.

THE INDUSTRIAL RECYCLING PARK

From today's perspective, dry fuel and pyrolysis are technologies which can convert a major expense into an economic benefit. By themselves, energy recovery technologies, however, have the disadvantages of burning already manufactured products as a fuel, and then shipping the energy product. Resource managers should be able to locate a series of technologies at a single site which can make the most efficient use of recovered materials and energy products.

We call this group of agglomerated and interrelated technologies the industrial recycling park. At this time, the
recycling park is a common-sense step beyond the energy recovery park -- one which has received little attention.
Nevertheless the pervasive logic of the idea and the availability of more than 40,000 TPD of waste in the Meadowlands
argues for a brief review of the industrial recycling
park.

The park would consist of one or more energy recovery
facilities, utilizing technologies which could make use of
recovered paper, steel, glass, and nonferrous metals, as
well as provide a complementary energy load for the recovery
facilities and the manufacturing facilities. Preliminary
work with the concept (Chapter 6) has identified the following facilities as likely candidates for a planned recycling
park.

1.   Energy: pyrolysis; dry fuel; water wall in-
     cineration.

2.   Light ferrous: detinning.

3.   Heavy ferrous: mini-steel mill producing steel
     reinforcing rods.

4.   Nonferrous: aluminum, copper, zinc, lead.

5.   Paper: newsprint (with front-end separation),
     corrugated.

6.   Glass: bottles, glass wool, glasphalt, glass
     brick, ceramic panels.

Residential waste, perhaps supplemented by industrial
waste, auto hulls, and other resource products, would be
brought to the facility for separation and shredding. Site
requirements are estimated to be about 100 acres. Transportation requirements include excellent access to major
interchanges,miles of railroad track, and direct access for
barge traffic. Discussions with industrial personnel suggest that the cost of the park could range from $150 to
$500 million.

We would expect the industrial recycling park to in-
duce further economic activity through secondary industries
and service activities. While it might spur economic activity, we are exploring the possible disadvantages of the
recycling park, including environmental impacts and negative
socioeconomic effects.

Theoretically, a cost effectiveness model for the recycling park can be designed. The objective would be to
minimize the size of the facility subject to constraints
on waste input, environmental degradation, capital and
operating costs, and recovered product and energy demands.
The model could be designed to pick an industrial mix under
conditions of alternative prices for materials and energy
products.

Overall, the industrial recycling park is not a technology of the immediate future. Ultimately it does offer
a common-sense step beyond energy recovery, a step which
can make more efficient use of residential solid waste than
landfilling or energy recovery.

LANDFILLING

Although this study is primarily concerned with the
application of resource recovery technoloy to solid waste
management in northern New Jersey, it must be recognized
that the dominant means of refuse disposal in this region
is presently by land disposal. A major commitment to resource recovery has not as yet been made. Landfilling will
continue in some form to be the singular method of refuse
disposal for the forseeable future. This section is divided into
three parts: (1) a description of present and proposed
methods of sanitary landfill operations; (2) a presentation
of future landfill costs; (3) a review of the major technical and policy issues affecting the application of the maximum landfill strategy in northern New Jersey.

It has been previously noted (Chapter 2) that the remaining capacity of most existing regional landfills in
the study area is rapidly being depleted and that major new
landfills developed in the Hackensack Meadowlands or elsewhere in northern New Jersey will be needed to provide adequate replacement capacity before 1980.

Present methods of refuse disposal will not be adequate
to meet increasingly rigorous air and water pollution control standards recently adopted in the state. Accordingly,
new landfills in northern New Jersey are expected to require
much greater capital investments in land and other on-site
improvement needed to protect environmental quality and
ensure safe operations. Operating costs for larger equipment,
skilled labor, engineering supervision, and additional cover
material are also expected to increase. The total amount
and timing of these increases are not yet known. The addition of volume reduction techniques such as refuse baling
or shredding prior to landfilling may also be added to extend
the operating lives of these new landfills and improve their
efficiency. These additional systems are also expected to

ll costs and development strategies. As new
..e needed, their location in the Hackensack
..ands or in other areas of the study region may also
..erge as a major solid waste management decision for the
region.

Because of these potential changes in the region's present solid waste management systems and the choice between
land disposal and resource recovery, the study team undertook
an evaluation of alternative landfill strategies for northern
New Jersey. This evaluation was designed to assess the impacts
of selected changes in the present regional landfill system,
particularly those resulting from the following: the application of higher pollution control standards; the addition of
volume reduction techniques to landfilling; and the choices
between the continuation of the present pattern of regional
landfilling in the Hackensack Meadowlands or the development
of alternative regional landfills in other areas of the study
region. The study was especially designed to provide economic
benchmarks for the continuation of this maximum landfill strategy against which alternative resource recovery strategies
could be compared.

Landfill Operations

The process of sanitary landfilling is an engineering
construction project for the burial of solid waste at the
optimum compaction in sealed cells of earth, designed to
produce a minimum impact on the environment, with a pre-
conceived plan for future development.[46] The American Society of Civil Engineers defines sanitary landfilling as
a method of disposal of refuse on land without creating
nuisances or hazards to public health and safety, utilizing
the principles of engineering to confine the refuse to the
smallest practical volume, and to cover it with a layer of
earth at the conclusion of each day's operation, or at such
more frequent intervals as may be necessary.[47] Although
substantial improvements have been made in recent years,
only a few of northern New Jersey's existing regional landfills fully comply with this definition. Future landfills,
however will have to comply with increasingly specific, rigorous, and potentially expensive state standards of engineering design, operation, and development to ensure that these
new facilities at least will provide safe and sanitary solid
waste disposal. The following is a brief discussion of the
principal elements of sanitary landfill operations and some
of the standards affecting the design and development of
such facilities in northern New Jersey.

The process of sanitary landfilling of solid waste consists of the following six operations: (1) refuse receiving,
(2) spreading and compaction, (3) covering, (4) site maintenance and vector control, (5) environmental protection,
and (6) site development and reuse. In addition, shredding
or baling refuse prior to landfilling may be added with some
modification in the overall process. Shredding and baling
operations are discussed later in this section.

Refuse Receiving

Solid waste entering the sanitary landfill passes
through a controlled access point where its weight or volume
is measured and its carrier identified for billing purposes.
New Jersey regulations now require all new landfills to
include truck scales for this purpose.[48] Weighing incoming
refuse helps the operator to monitor and control daily operations and provides additional information on collection patterns and the quantities and seasonal variations in refuse
generation.

After weighing and billing, the refuse is carried in
the collection vehicle directly to the disposal area where
it is discharged. Smaller quantities of solid waste may also
be deposited at common containers at the landfill entrance to
reduce vehicle traffic and potential damage to private automobiles and small trucks.

This phase of landfill operations may take 15 to 30
minutes to complete, depending on truck volume, size of
operating area, and road conditions. Any or all of these
conditions may vary substantially from day to day. Private
refuse collectors appear to be very sensitive to the amount
of time required for this nonproductive operation and commonly
shift operations to other landfills when turn-around time
becomes excessive.[49]

Spreading and Compaction

A major objective of sanitary landfill operation is to
reduce the volume of the incoming refuse to the smallest
practical size. This is commonly accomplished by the use
of large track-mounted dozers, rubber-tired tractors, or
special landfill compactors. These vehicles spread the refuse in layers less than two feet thick and make three to
five passes over the waste prior to covering. New Jersey
state regulations require a minimum compacted density of
700 pounds per cubic yard of refuse.[50] Refuse densities of
800 to 1,200 pounds per cubic yard are commonly achieved at

some landfills. Good refuse spreading and compaction reduces
the amount of land and cover material required as well as the
amount of settlement which may occur after landfill operations
are complete. Greater compaction and spreading also reduce
the hazard of refuse fires and destroy potential harborage
for rats and other rodents normally attracted to landfills.
Successive layers of compacted refuse may be combined into
lifts of not more than 12 feet high before covering.[51] The
total height of individual landfills may range up to 80 or 100
feet, depending on the size and terrain of the disposal site.
At present, there are no state regulations governing the height
of landfills.

Covering

Perhaps the single most important phase of sanitary landfill operations is the selection and application of cover
material. Some of the most common distinctions between an
unsanitary dump and a sanitary landfill can be attributed to
the lack of proper cover.   The daily application of at
least six inches of impervious soil cover over the compacted
refuse reduces offensive odors and flying paper, prevents
rats and birds from feeding on the refuse, and reduces the potential for refuse fires.

The regular application of an impervious soil cover also
prevents surface water from infiltrating through the landfill, which commonly produces erosion and water pollution.
The recommended soil cover for this purpose is sandy loam
(45 to 80 percent sand, the balance of silt or clay) although
many other less impervious soil types are commonly used.[52]
For maximum effectiveness, however, cover must be applied
daily to all active landfill areas and should be properly compacted and graded to prevent erosion or ponding of surface
water.

State regulations require that all landfills provide
daily cover over all exposed surfaces and that the active
disposal area be limited to a maximum of 15,000 square feet
(approximately one-third acre).[53] Additional intermediate
cover is required for areas to be exposed longer than 24
hours, and two feet of final cover must be added to all areas
to be exposed for longer than six months.[54]

Site Maintenance

Site maintenance and vector control are routine and in-
tegral elements in sanitary landfill operations. The activities include grading, surfacing, and repairing on-site
roads, collecting litter, regrading and covering breaks in the

landfill surface or side slope, planting grass or other
ground cover to prevent erosion and maintaining entrance
gates, perimeter fencing, and buildings. Vector control programs include baiting to prevent rats and other rodents from
inhibiting the landfill, seasonal spraying to suppress
flies and other insects, and special (often futile) efforts
to control birds. These maintenance activities, like daily
cover, are a common distinction between a dump and a sanitary landfill.

Environmental Protection

Two major sources of environmental pollution are typically associated with landfilling solid waste. These include surface and groundwater pollution from leachate for-
mation and the production of volatile gases.

Groundwater or infiltrating surface water moving through
the landfill can produce leachate, a liquid solution containing dissolved and finally suspended solids and microbial waste
products generated by the decomposition of the organic material in the refuse. This leachate may leave the landfill
at the surface or through the sides of the fill or through
the bottom of the landfill into nearby groundwater. The production rate and exact composition of leachate is highly
variable, depending primarily on the composition of the refuse,
the amount of water entering and leaving the landfill, and
the physical, chemical, and biological activities of refuse
settlement and decomposition. Exhibit 7.15 contains a summary of some of the major constitutents of leachate in comparison with raw sewage of medium strength and potable water
standards. When present in sufficient quantities and concentrations, leachate can degrade surface and ground water
quality and potability at considerable distances from the
landfill.

EXHIBIT 7.15 [a]

WATER QUALITY OF LEACHATE

Component	Leachate	Sewage	Potable Water
Iron	1,600	-	0.3
Hardness [b]	2,500	-	150
Suspended Solids	750	300	1
Total Solids	10,000 to 28,000	500	-
Biochemical Oxygen Demand (BOD)	25,000	200	-

[a]All units are milligrams per liter (mg/l).
[b]As measured in calcium carbonate.
Source: F. Flower, "The Refuse Landfill," Executive Housekeeper
Vol. 22, No.2, February 1974, p.24.

Leachate control measures include daily cover and upland diversion ditches to prevent surface water from entering the landfill, impervious liners and dikes to prevent leachate from entering adjacent surface and groundwater, and on-site leachate collection and treatment systems. Impervious liners such as clay, asphalt, plastic, and bentonite can be installed on new landfills at increased capital and operating costs. On-site treatment may include biological, chemical, and physical methods. It is also possible to incorporate the processes of any existing sewage treatment plant into the leachate treatment system following on-site pretreatment.

The production of volatile gases particularly methane and carbon dioxide, are a common by-product of the decomposition of organic refuse in the absence of oxygen. As with leachate, the quantity and composition of gases vary with the type of refuse landfilled, particularly the amount of organic matter, the amount of moisture in the fill, and the rate of decomposition. The control of landfill gas can be a major problem in sanitary landfill operations because methane is explosive at concentrations between 5 and 15 percent, and mineralization of groundwater can occur if carbon dioxide dissolves to form carbonic acid.[55]

Methane is lighter than oxygen. Accordingly, it may move through the landfill into pockets of uncompacted refuse or through surrounding porous soils into basements of buildings on or near the landfills. Landfill fires or explosions due to the concentration of landfill gases have occurred in many areas of the country and in New Jersey. Smaller concentrations of landfill gases have also killed grasses, shrubs, and trees on landfills and an adjacent properties.[56]

The concentration and movement of landfill gases can be prevented by the efficient compaction of refuse within the landfill, placing impermeable barriers or gravel-filled trenches around the fill, or placing vent pipes into the landfill through a relatively impermeable top cover.

New sanitary landfills in New Jersey will be required to comply with increasingly rigorous environmental protection standards for the prevention or control of leachate and landfill gases. In addition to daily cover, a minimum compaction, and regular site maintenance, new landfills will be required to include specific plans and facilities for the control of leachate, groundwater monitoring wells, the provision of gas monitoring and venting systems, and the maintenance of a 50 foot buffer strip between the landfill and adjacent property.[57] Many existing landfills in the state are also being required to install these pollution control measures.

Site Development and Reuse

Most landfills in New Jersey are considered by their owners and operators as land reclamation projects designed to produce usable land for future development and reuse. To date the most common uses of completed refuse landfills are as parks, playgrounds, golf courses, parking lots, storage yards, and as sites for the construction of light-weight buildings.

Where engineers, site operators, and developers re-cognize potential problems of landfill settlement, subsur-face corrosion, and gas production, it is possible to con-struct larger buildings on refuse landfills; construction costs however, are often substantially greater than those for building on unfilled land. The load-bearing capacity of refuse landfills is low, highly variable, and relatively unknown. The corrosiveness of landfill soil may destroy subsurface utilities. Landfill settlement, which often con-tinues for a number of years, may require expensive re-pairs and maintenance to building foundations, parking lots, and roads. Buildings must also be located and designed to prevent landfill gases from entering basements and working areas. As previously noted, grass, trees, and shrubs may also be affected by landfill gas and so require increased care and replacement.

In short, to avoid these problems and achieve their reuse objectives, sanitary landfills must be carefully located, designed, and operated; and they must include all necessary environmental protection measures and conform to a specific reuse plan.

Shredding

Shredding solid waste involves the mechanical breaking, shearing, or tearing of the raw refuse to reduce the size of the resulting particles and to increase the uniformity and density of the final product. Common terms associated with this process include shredding, grinding, pulverizing, milling and shearing.[58]

Shredding may be used to process selected portions of the waste stream such as white goods, paper and metal products, and automobiles, or it can be used to treat all types of municipal refuse brought to the processing plant. Shredding may also be combined with material recovery processes, such as magnetic metals recovery, to produce system revenue and reduce the quantity of refuse requiring final disposal. Nearly all energy and material recovery systems include shredding as an initial processing step. Shredding is also in common use in some industrial processes and by the secondary materials in-dustry to improve the uniformity, density and handling quali-ties of the material processed.

~cent years, shredding municipal solid waste has
.. combined with sanitary landfilling operations in a
number of communities in this country and in Canada. This
combined processing and disposal system in presently practiced in some communities including, Madison, Wisconsin;
Milford, Connecticut; St. Catherine's, Ontario; and Pompano
Beach, Florida. A shredding-and-landfill operation is
scheduled to shortly begin in Monmouth County, New Jersey.

Combined shredding and landfill systems generally include the following unit processes: raw refuse receiving
and storage; primary materials separation (hand picking);
shredding; secondary materials recovery (i.e., ferrous metals,
dry fuel), compaction and transportation, and final land
disposal. The shredding operation may occur at the landfill
or at a centralized processing facility with the shredded
refuse being transported to a more remote landfill. At the
landfill, final disposal may or may not include the use of
cover materials.

Operating capacities for a shredding plant may range
from 100 tons per day to 1000 tons per day depending on the
number and size of the shredders and the number of operating
shifts per day. Due to the need to regularly repair and replace shredder components, shredding plants are designed to
operate on one - or two-shift bases with the remaining shift
used for routing maintenance. Shredding is generally accepted
as a proven and reliable method of processing municipal solid
waste for resource recovery and improved landfill operations.

The final product of the shredding process is a relatively homogeneous material with most particles less than 2 to 5
inches in size. Since paper is the largest single component
in municipal refuse, the general appearance and texture of
shredded refuse is that of a coarse confetti. Putrescible
materials and moisture are generally distributed and absorbed
throughout the mass. Metal cans are crumpled or sliced into
smaller particles, and glass is disintegrated and diffused
throughout the material. When combined with sanitary landfilling, shredding municipal solid waste can produce a number
of significant operating and esthetic benefits. Some of the
most important of these are listed below:[59]

1.   Increasing landfill density. Because of its
      increased density and compactability, 35 to 50
      percent less space may be required to landfill
      shredded refuse without cover than with conven-
      tional landfilling. Average in-place densities
      of shredded refuse may range from 1,200 to 1,500
      pounds per cubic yard.

2.   Shredded refuse can be landfilled without daily
      or intermittent cover and still meet sanitary
      landfill standards. Where cover is required,
      less cover is needed and a greater variety of
      soil may be used. The limited use of cover re-
      duces operating costs and landfill capacity re-
      quirements.

3.   The use of shredded refuse may also increase
      operating efficiency and reduce operating costs
      through easier refuse handling and compaction,
      reducing tire punctures and equipment damage,
      and by reducing the amount of paper and dust
      blowing about.

4.   Fire hazards are reduced. Although freshly
      shredded refuse does support a fire, the fire
      spreads slowly and is readily extinguished with
      water. Densely compacted shredded refuse also
      prevents the formation of voids within the land-
      fill where gas accumulation and spontaneous com-
      bustion can occur.

5.   Rats, flies, and other disease-carrying vectors
      cannot survive for extended periods of time be-
      cause of the rapid decomposition of the putres-
      cible portions of shredded refuse.

These benefits have been identified from actual operating experience at several "shreddfill" operations. In recent years the most notable of these has been in Madison,
Wisconsin.

It should be noted, however, that uncovered shredded
refuse appears to produce leachate earlier and with higher
concentrations of contaminants than conventional landfills
employing daily cover.[60] This may be a detriment to the
widespread disposal of shredded refuse without cover in New
Jersey. However, it also appears that once the peak period
of leachate production passes, shredded refuse landfills
tend to produce less water-born pollution than conventional
landfills.[61] Research into this problem is continuing. The
shreddfill operation in Monmouth County will not include
daily cover. If water pollution problems occur daily cover
will be applied. Estimated operating costs for refuse shredding and landfilling range from $3 to $7 per ton, depending
upon the type and size of the operation.[62] Capital costs for
the shredding facilities range from $1.2 million for a 250-ton-
per-day plant to $8.5 million for a 3000-ton-per-day plant.[63]

Baling

Baling solid waste prior to landfilling may also be used to reduce its volume and the land area required for refuse disposal. Landfilling baled refuse may also facilitate the early reclamation and reuse of the disposal site for other purposes.

The baling process is designed to compress solid wastes mechanically and bind it into blocklike shapes having a density of between 1,600 and 2,000 pounds per cubic yard. As a result, less land is required for landfill purposes and the operating life of existing landfills may be extended. In addition, since there is virtually no settlement, baled refuse can be stacked in patterns and heights approximating the final site design -- and reuse can occur immediately upon completion.[64]

Unit operations involved in landfilling baled refuse generally consist of refuse weighing, receiving and storage, baling/binding, transportation to the landfill, and placement and cover. Baling operations may be preceded by shredding and/or materials recovery processes involving shredding and magnetic metals recovery.

A typical baling system presently in operation in St. Paul, Minnesota, works in this way: The baling plant includes a dumping floor, conveyor systems, and a single three-stroke baler. The plant presently processes about 500 tons of refuse per eight-hour day. It has the potential to process 1,000 tons per day using a double-shift operation.

The plant is almost completely automated. The refuse is received on the dumping floor, pushed onto the conveyor system with a front-end loader, and charged into the baler by a gravity-feed system. The completed bales are automatically discharged onto a flat-bed truck for transport to a landfill about 12 miles away. The reported average density of the bales is about 1,800 pounds per cubic yard.[65]

At the landfill one front-end loader equipped with a fork mechanism is used to unload the bales and place them in the site. The bales are covered with dirt at the end of each day's operation. Three workers are employed at the baling plant and one at the landfill. The costs of baling and landfilling are estimated to be between $7 and $8 per ton.[66] These costs are comparable to shredding-and-landfill operations and are approximately 2.5 times present landfill costs. They are almost double the estimated cost of new sanitary landfills in the study area. The principal advantage of this system, as with shredding, is in improved land conservation and reclamation and in reducing the esthetic impact of conservation landfilling.

Landfill Costs

The average unit costs for solid waste disposal at major regional landfills in northern and central New Jersey are shown below:

EXHIBIT 7.16

CURRENT LANDFILL COSTS

Area	*Dollars Per Ton*
Hackensack Meadowlands	$2.40 to $2.80
Bergen County	2.80 to 3.00
Morris and Middlesex Counties	2.00 to 3.28

The cost in the immediate future is not clear. On the one hand, new and more stringent environmental protection standards of the type previously noted could increase these average prices to approximately $8 per ton within five years.[67] Smaller landfills with more limited refuse volumes could incur even greater cost increases.[68] As previously noted, the cost of combining refuse shredding and baling with landfilling could increase present costs to $7 or $8 per ton.

On the other hand, although present landfill costs and refuse disposal prices are expected to increase as a result of these standards and general inflationary pressures, two factors may delay the dramatic increases. First, as older and environmentally unsound landfills close, remaining landfills will receive proportionately larger refuse quantities, thus increasing revenues and the economics of operating. Up to a point, these increases should make it economically possible to install pollution control systems without requiring increases in disposal charges. Major pollution control investments will probably not be made on landfills with remaining operating lives too short to recoup these costs.

In addition, major investments in pollution control facilities may not be feasible or effective at some landfills because of prior intensive site development or other physical limitations. In these cases, actual investments may be limited to monitoring systems, improved operating practices -- for example, added cover, increased compaction, better grading and drainage -- without producing major increases in present unit costs.

Overall, refuse disposal costs and prices at existing regional landfills in northern New Jersey may remain relatively stable or rise slowly during the near term. Environmental quality near these facilities may not substantially improve. Major changes in cost and environmental quality should be expected with new, regional landfills.

The capital and operating costs for new sanitary landfills of various operating scales in northern New Jersey were obtained by udating and regionalizing national average landfill costs developed by the Midwest Research Institute for the Council on Environmental Quality.[69] These estimates were further compared with other cost data contained in specific landfill proposals and plans within the study area.

Estimated capital costs range from slightly over $1 million at the 250-ton-per-day operating level to $7.3 million at the 2,000-ton-per-day level. Unit costs range from $4.39 per ton for the smallest facility to $3.82 per ton for the largest. It should be noted that most regional landfills in northern New Jersey presently operate at levels above 1,000 tons per day.

These initial cost estimates assume that new sanitary landfills will comply with all environmental protection standards presently in effect and will be developed and operated by a public agency such as a county or municipal department using general obligation bond financing. However, New Jersey has a well-developed private solid waste disposal industry, and potentially strong public and industry opposition to new publicly owned landfills is likely to prevent counties or municipalities from undertaking such regional projects.

Therefore, these basic cost estimates were modified further to reflect the capital and operating costs associated with private landfill development and operation. These private landfill costs (Exhibit 7.17) range from 20 to 25 percent higher than public operations, owing primarily to higher capital charges, taxes, and other overhead costs and profits.

EXHIBIT 7.17

CAPITAL AND OPERATING COSTS OF NEW REGIONAL LANDFILLS

	Operating Level, Tons Per Day			
	250	500	1,000	2,000
Capital costs	3.33	3.18	3.00	2.74
Operating Costs	2.15	2.07	2.01	1.84
Total Cost	5.48	5.25	5.01	4.58

   The unit cost of private landfill operations range from
a high of $5.48 per ton for the smaller-scale operation to
$4.58 for the largest. These cost are approximately 50 per-
cent greater than present landfill prices in the study area.
These cost estimates were used by the study team to to eval-
uate alternative solid waste management systems for northern
New Jersey.

   In addition to the basic landfilling costs, the estimated
cost of large-scale refuse baling and landfilling were also
included in this analysis, together with the estimated cost
of rail-hauling of refuse out of the study area to
disposal sites in central or southern New Jersey. The estimated unit costs of these alternatives are $7 per ton and
$10 per ton,respectively.[70]

POLICY CONSIDERATIONS

   The Hackensack Meadowlands Development Commission
(HMDC) has advised municipalities in northern New Jersey that
existing landfills within the Meadowlands district will not
last longer than two or three additional years at present
operating levels.[71] The recent prohibition by the Commission
of out-of-state refuse disposal within the district and
the planned addition of new landfill capacity in selected
areas of the Meadowlands are not expected to prevent the
bulk of this area's present landfill capacity from being consumed before 1980. As previously noted by 1980, only a hand-
full of existing landfill sites outside the Meadowlands district are likely to be available to provide an alternative
refuse disposal capacity for the northern New Jersey region. In short, if the maximum landfill strategy is to continue the development of new regional landfills will be
needed in the very near future to meet the region's solid
waste disposal needs. Indeed, even under a maximum resource
recovery strategy, new regional landfill will also be needed
to: (1) provide adequate interim disposal capacity while
the resource recovery systems are being developed; (2) provide safe, efficient disposal capacity for solid waste, primarily industrial refuse, that cannot be feasibly or safely
processed by present recovery technology; and (3) provide
disposal capacity for the residue of resource recovery operations which may range from 10 to 30 percent of the refuse
processes.

   Northern New Jersey's future landfill needs may be
met through two general development strategies:

   1.   Additional land within the Hackensack Meadowlands
        may be committed to landfilling, using either

conventional sanitary landfill methods or the addition of shredding and/or baling systems.

2.   New sanitary landfills may be developed in other areas of the study region outside the Meadowlands or in other areas of the state through the expansion of existing landfills or the development of completely new facilities.

The future expansion of northern New Jersey's present landfill system or the development of new sanitary landfills will be much more difficult, time consuming, and expensive than the construction of the region's existing landfills due to a number of recent developments. First, there is strong and persistent public opposition to the development of new landfills anywhere in the state. Whether for esthetic, economic, or political reasons such opposition has been effective in defeating or postponing regional landfill proposals in Union, Somerset, Mercer, and other counties and in the Meadowlands. Local public opposition reduces the chances of even the best landfill proposal.

Secondly, increasingly rigorous and detailed standards for environmental protection will extend the lead time required for state review and approval of new landfill designs. Next, as indicated above, the implementation of suitable environmental protection measures will increase both the capital and the operating costs of new or expanded landfills. The addition of refuse shredding and/or baling systems to prolong operating life and improve environmental quality will also increase disposal costs and prices.

Finally, it will become increasingly difficult and expensive to find and acquire land suitable for large sanitary landfill operations. Large tracts of relatively inexpensive wetlands or other "wasteland" are not as abundant as in former times and also have much higher environmental and economic values. Undeveloped residential and other urban land may be unavailable for similar reasons. Accordingly, new sanitary landfills may have to compete for smaller tracts of prime industrial land as suitable locations at increased costs. The limited amounts and increased cost of suitable landfill sites should slow the replacement process and will increase the overall cost of landfilling in the study area after 1980.

To provide a realistic structure for evaluating the economic and locational choices inherent in this maximum landfill strategy, the study team considered three major issues:

(1) the number and operating scale of future
     landfills;
(2) the probable size and operating life of
     future sites; and
(3) the locations and accessibility of future
     landfills.

At present there are 51 regional scale landfills in the
northern New Jersey study area, 18 of which are located
within the Hackensack Meadowlands district. All of these
18 landfills are expected to reach capacity before 1980 or
shortly thereafter. Due to probable strong public opposition, increased costs, and higher environmental standards
associated with the development of any new landfills, it is
likely that only a limited number of new landfills will be
developed within the study area to provide replacement capacity.

As a result, the design capacity of individual new
landfills is likely to be at least as large as or greater
than, the largest existing landfills. The actual operating
capacity for these sites will be largely determined by their
number and the amount of refuse requiring disposal, their
relative proximity to centers of refuse production, and the
relative disposal and transport costs to competing facilities
within the study area and in adjacent counties. The accessibility of individual sites to the regional road network may
also play an important part in controlling their operating
level, since refuse haulers tend to avoid lost time caused
by raod congestion and long turn-around times.

In recognition of these potential conditions, the study
team initially assumed that new regional scale landfills
with design capacities of 2,000 tons per day would be established after 1980 and that these new facilities would be
established in the Hackensack Meadowlands district or at
other locations in the study area as the centralized and
dispersed landfill strategies, respectively. Subsequent
tests, reviewed in Chapter 8 led us to isolate a few cases
where smaller scale facilities appear to be justified.

Under the centralized strategy it was further assumed
that existing landfills in the district would be upgraded
and expanded to provide increased capacity and operating
scale, or that refuse baling or shredding facilities would
be included as elements of new landfill projects. The
economic impact of these alternatives, together with the
rail-hauling of refuse out of the district, were evaluated
in successive computer runs. Similar-scale landfills were
considered in testing the dispersed landfill pattern. However, volume reduction technologies(baling and shredding options

and rail-haul)were not included.

The probable size and operating life of these new land-fills will depend on the amount and type of land that can be acquired for this purpose, their respective operating capacities, and the relative efficiency of the land disposal operation. In order to amortize capital investments in equipment, on-site improvements, and environmental protection measures, a minimum operating life should be at least 10 years. To reduce the long-term economic and community development impact of landfill operations on neighboring areas, the landfills should probably not operate longer than 10 or 15 years. The staged redevelopment of completed portions should occur as soon as conditions permit. The new landfills may require 150 to 250 acres each in order to provide adequate disposal capacity for this period and ensure adequate buffer zones between adjacent properties.

The location of new regional landfills in northern New Jersey, particularly under the dispersed pattern, is perhaps the most difficult issue raised by the maximum landfill strategy. Officials were unable to offer any sites or even guidelines. In an attempt to resolve this issue within the context of this regional study the study team employed the following methodology for locating the hypothetical land-fills used in this analysis. First, in the absence of a regional solution, we assumed that each county might be a solid waste planning unit. Accordingly, an attempt was made to find at least one (and up to three) 2,000 TPD landfill sites in each of the five regional counties and the neighboring counties: Bergen, Essex, Hudson, Passaic, Union, Morris, Somerset, and Middlesex.

Within each of these counties, one guideline was used for choosing potential communities. The requirement was that the community should have at least 200 acres zoned for industrial use in order to meet the size requirement. Second, we required the community to have access to one or more interstate or county roads in order to meet accessibility constraints. When many communities in a county met the requirements, we eliminated those that were the farthest distance from the Hackensack region's population.

As indicated in Chapter 2, individual sites, within communities were not chosen and the economic, social, and environmental of individual communities were not investigated. Clearly, specific landfill-site selection is itself a major project far beyond the scope of this study. In essence, the seven dispersed landfill sites we ultimately picked,represent approximations of where regional landfill sites might be placed on the basis of general operating rules. The mathematical model is used in Chapter 8 to test the economic effectiveness of these landfill locations with respect to each other and with respect to the alternative resource recovery technology/site combinations.

NOTES

1.   See R.A. Colonna and C. McLaren, <u>Decision-Makers Guide</u>
      <u>in Solid Waste Management</u> (Washington, D.C.: U.S.EPA,
      1974) for a brief comparison of the advantages and dis-
      advantages of incineration. See Midwest Research In-
      stitute, <u>Resource Recovery: The State of Technology</u>
      (Washington, D.C.: Council of Environmental Quality,
      1973) for another comparison.

2.   State of New Jersey, County and Municipal Government
      Study Commission, <u>Solid Waste</u> (Trenton, N.J., 1972),
      pp. 30, 40.

3.   See H.W. Schulz, <u>A Pollution-Free System for the</u>
      <u>Economic Utilization of Municipal Solid Waste for the</u>
      <u>City of New York,</u> (New York: Columbia University,
      April 1973),and Midwest Research Institute, 1973.

4.   Robert Lowe, <u>Energy Recovery from Waste</u> (Washington,
      D.C.: U.S. EPA, 1973), p.7.

5.   <u>Ibid.</u>, p.3.

6.   Richard E. Hopper, <u>A Nationwide Survey of Resource</u>
      <u>Recovery Activities</u>, (Washington, D.C.: U.S. EPA,
      January 1975), p. 45.

7.   The General Electric Company and the State of Connect-
      icut, Department of Environmental Protection, <u>A Plan</u>
      <u>of Solid Waste Management for Connecticut</u> (Hartford,
      1973), p.41.

8.   Hopper, <u>op.cit.</u>, pp. 46-47.

9.   <u>Ibid.</u>, various pages.

10.   <u>Ibid.</u>, p.6.

11.   V. Angkatavanich, <u>et al.</u>, <u>An Analysis of Solid Waste</u>
      <u>Processing Proposals for the Hackensack Meadowlands</u>
      <u>Development Commission</u> (Hackensack: Fairleigh Dickin-
      son University and Stevens Institute of Technology,
      September 1973), p.1.

12.   William McDowell, executive director, Hackensack
      Meadowlands Development Commission, interview, May
      14, 1975.

13. Horner and Shifrin, consulting engineers, "Appraisal of Use of Solid Waste as Supplemetal Fuel in Power Plant Boilers," New York, the City of New York, Environmental Protection Administration, February 1973, pp. iii-iv.

14. Ibid.

15. From Angkatavanich, op. cit. pp. 45-48.

16. Where the Boilers Are, A Survey of Electric Utility Boilers with Potential Capacity for Burning Solid Waste as Fuel (Washington, D.C., U.S. Office of Solid Waste Management Programs, 1974), p.3.

17. Ibid.

18. Ibid., pp. 16-17.

19. Regional Energy Consumption, Second Interim Report, Regional Plan Association, Inc. and Resources for the Future, Inc.(New York, 1974), Table 13, p.34.

20. Low estimate is drawn from Horner and Shrifin, op.cit., Table 5, and represents the average estimated cost of converting nine Con Edison boilers to accommodate refuse fuel. On-site fuel-receiving and storage and firing facilities are also included. The high estimate was derived by the study team by adding 50 percent to these previous cost estimates. Estimates for individual boilers -- New Jersey -- have been as high as $3.75 to 5.0 million (see Angkatavanich, et al., op.cit., p. 98). Without detailed study, all cost estimates in this area must be considered speculative.

21. Robert Lowe., op.cit.

22. These estimates were updated to northern New Jersey from national average estimates for 1971 contained in Resource Recovery Technology, the State of the Art prepared for the Council on Environmental Quality by the Midwest Research Institute, February 1973.

23. Horner and Shrifrin, op.cit., p. iv.

24. Robert Lowe, op.cit., p. 18.

25. F.O.B. New York Barges. All prices from Oil and Gas Journal, January 1973 and May 1974, respectively.

26. David B. Sussman, <u>Baltimore Demonstrates Gas Pyrolysis</u>, first interim report (Washington, D.C.: U.S.EPA 1975),p.14.

27. <u>Ibid.</u>, p.5.

28. <u>Ibid.</u>, p.8.

29. <u>Ibid.</u>, p.14.

30. <u>Ibid.</u>, p.20.

31. <u>Ibid.</u>, p.2.

32. Steven J. Levy, <u>Pyrolysis of Municipal Solid Waste</u> U.S. EPA, (Washington, D.C.: (1973) unpublished memorandum, p. 12.

33. <u>Ibid.</u>, p.15

34. <u>Ibid.</u>, p.18.

35. <u>Ibid.</u>, p.13.

36. <u>Ibid.</u>, p.15.

37. <u>Ibid.</u>, p.18.

38. H.W. Schulz and R. Lyford-Pike, <u>A Solid Waste Utiliza-tion Plan for Westchester County, New York</u> (New York: Columbia University and National Science Foundation RANN, September 1974), p.15.

39. <u>Ibid.</u>, p.16.

40. Schulz, <u>op.cit.</u>

41. Communication from Mr. James Steinhagen, September 1975.

42. Levy, <u>op.cit.</u>, p.9.

43. <u>Ibid.</u>, p.11.

44. <u>Ibid.</u>, p.11.

45. Schulz, <u>op.cit.</u>, p.32.

46. <u>Middlesex County Solid Waste Management Program</u>,Vol.I: Comprehensive Report, Middlesex County, New Brunswick N.J. (1974) p. 11-1.

47. Committee on Sanitary Landfill Practice of the Sanitary Engineering Division, *Sanitary Landfill*, ASCE Manual of Engineering Practice, No. 39, American Society of Civil Engineers (1959).

48. Rules of the Bureau of Solid Waste Management NJAC 7:26-1 *et sq.*, New Jersey Department of Environmental Protection, Trenton (July 1, 1974), section 2.5.25.

49. Middlesex County, *op.cit.* pp. 12-16.

50. Rules, *op.cit.*, section 2.5.2.

51. *Ibid.*, Section 2.5.3.

52. F. Flower, "The Refuse Landfill" *Executive Housekeeper,* Vol.22, No.2, February 1974, p.24.

53. *Rules, op.cit.* section 2.5.13.

54. *Ibid.*, section 2.5.14-15.

55. Dirk R. Brunner and Daniel J. Killer, *Sanitary Landfill Design and Operating* (Washington, D.C.: U.S. EPA, 1972),p.7.

56. F. Flower "Ultimate Use of Completed Refuse Landfills" *Air Pollution Notes,* Vol. 8, No. 3, May 1974, p.2.

57. Rules, *op.cit.* sections 2.5.21-22 and 2.12.2,respectively.

58. Middlesex County, *op.cit.*, p. 14-1.

59. *Ibid.*, p. 14-7.

60. Robert K. Ham, Warner K. Pattes, and John J. Reinhardt, "Refuse Milling for Landfill Disposal," in *Public Works* February 1972, p.16.

61. *Ibid.*, p.16.

62. *Decision-Makers'Guide*, *op.cit.*, p.86.

63. Middlesex County, *op.cit.*, p. 14-13.

64. *Ibid.*, p. 15-6.

65. *Ibid.*, p.15-1.

66. *Decision-Makers' Guide*, *op.cit.*, p. 83.

67. Horace J. De Podwin Statement before the New Jersey
     Department of Environmental Protection on the Economic
     Impacts of the Proposed Rules of the Bureau of Solid
     Waste, January 25, 1974, p. 3.

68. Ibid., p. 4.

69. Midwest Research Institute, Resource Recovery,The State
     of Technology,(Washington, D.C.: The Council on Environ-
     mental Quality, 1973), pp. 22-25.

70. V. Angkatavanich, et.al., op.cit. pp. 76, 77, and 83.

71. Ibid., p.5.

CHAPTER 8

SIMULATING THE REGIONAL SOLID
WASTE MANAGEMENT SYSTEM

This chapter reviews the simulation runs that lead us to the conclusion that resource recovery is a preferred technology to landfilling. While we have modeled only one region, we believe that this conclusion will be relevant to other urbanized regions which have felt the economic impact of increased energy costs and the environmental impact of landfilling and which face a shortage of inexpensive space for landfilling. The chapter is divided into five sections: (1) a summary of the components of the solid waste management system; (2) the costs of continuing the centralized landfilling strategy; (3) a dispersed, regional landfill strategy; (4) dry fuel recovery technology; and (5) gas pyrolysis recovery technology.

*A SUMMARY OF THE COMPONENTS OF THE SOLID
WASTE MANAGEMENT SYSTEM*

Chapters 4 through 7 have considered the sources of residential solid waste (Chapter 4), alternative transportation strategies for moving this waste (Chapter 5), markets for recovered products (Chapters 6 and 7), and technologies for making the best economic use of the solid waste (Chapter 7).

A brief summary of the most important facts developed in these chapters should help set the stage for the major conclusions and plethora of detail presented in this chapter.

The five-county study area produces about 46,000 tons of residential solid waste per week. Projections suggest that the weekly load will increase to about 53,000 tons in 1980 and 60,000 tons in 1985. Nearly all of this waste is hauled directly by trucks. Few communities have transfer stations. Our analysis of about 300 waste-source-to-facility paths indicates that transfer stations should become an important factor in regional solid waste management planning only if communities feel a need to make long hauls outside the region to the west and south in order to avoid increased disposal charges in the Hackensack Meadowlands.

Four major solid waste disposal technologies were found to be possible, if not acceptable, alternatives to meeting the study area's disposal problems from 1975 through 1985. The most obvious alternative is to continue to haul about 46,000 tons of waste each week to the Hackensack Meadowlands landfills. This practice has been recently curtailed due to the closing of some landfills in the Meadowlands. The Hackensack Meadowlands Commission plans to all but halt landfilling by 1980.

An alternative to hauling nearly all the waste to a centralized landfilling site is to landfill the solid waste at sites outside the Meadowlands. We have chosen representative sites in communities with excellent road access and large amounts of undeveloped industrial space. On the one hand, this landfill solution would greatly reduce the burden on the Meadowlands area, but would undoubtedly face opposition of the harshest form from the chosen communities.

The third alternative is a dry fuel technology which recovers an energy product and ferrous metals from the solid waste. Sixty percent of the waste is converted into a fuel which can be fired in utility boilers. About half the remaining solid waste is marketable recovered products and the remaining half should be landfilled. Both centralized and dispersed locations for these dry fuel facilities were chosen. The dry fuel option requires utility boiler alterations and may therefore not be an acceptable alternative to the utilities.

Gas pyrolysis is a fourth option. It does not require major utility alterations but is more expensive to construct and to operate. Pyrolysis recovers a gas product which can be piped to a utility generating station and a frit which may be sold. Best, medium, and worst revenue pictures are developed for both of the resource recovery options.

THE COSTS OF CONTINUING THE
CENTRALIZED LANDFILLING STRATEGY

Our analysis of the current centralized landfilling strategy indicates that the current landfill charge of between $2 and $4 per ton is grossly underpriced. The five important centralized landfilling simulations are summarized in Exhibit 8.1. We started by modeling the 1975 system with the hope that the results would validate the fact that the Meadowlands have been receiving between 40,000 and 46,000 tons of waste per week. Run 1 confirms this assumption by sending more than 40,000 of the region's 46,000 tons to the Meadowlands at a weekly, total system cost of almost $300,000. Run 1 also identifies the importance of transportation in the management of the solid waste system. Twenty-one of the 25 sheds send all of their waste to the Meadowlands landfills (Exhibit 8.2). Four do not. These four waste sheds lie at the periphery of the region and/or have existing transfer stations. While the optimization procedure assigns most of their waste to non-Meadowlands landfills, in reality the waste of three of the waste sheds is just as likely to go to the Meadowlands. The Mahwah waste shed lies in northwestern Bergen County. Our calculations find that it is $.27 per ton cheaper (3 percent) for these communities in this waste shed to send as much of their waste as possible to the Roxbury landfill and the remaining waste to the Meadowlands. The small difference between the Roxbury and Meadowland hauls implies that these communities are in reality just as likely to send their waste to the Meadowlands as to Morris County.

The cases of the Elizabeth (23) See [Exhibit 8.9 for waste shed numbers] and Westfield (24) waste sheds are even better examples of the indifference of the Meadowlands versus non Meadowlands choices. The Elizabeth waste shed sends all its waste to the Mount Olive landfill via a transfer station on the basis of a $.02 per ton difference in cost. The Westfield (24) shed's waste is allocated to Edison because of a $.03 per ton cost difference. Clearly these fractions of 1 percent difference in cost are unlikely to be recognized by carters and, indeed, may be due our inexact estimates of unit costs and transportation times.

Overall, only one of the 25 waste sheds (Summit-21) appears to have an obvious economic motivation to use its existing transfer station to avoid hauling waste to the Meadowlands.

The conclusion reached in the first run is mirrored by the 1980 simulation run. The same geographical assignments are made in Run 2 as in Run 1 (Exhibit 8.2). In short, the first two runs point to the unmistakable conclusion that the

EXHIBIT 8.1

ESTIMATED COSTS OF CONTINUING THE CENTRALIZED LANDFILLNG STRATEGY

Model Results	1	2	Run Number 3	4	5
Year	1975	1980	1980	1980	1980
Meadowlands[a] Cost,$ per ton	2.70	2.70	4.58	7.00	10.00
Total Cost ($1,000)	298	341	424	523	619
Haul Cost ($1,000) % of total	173 58	198 58	198 47	209 40	261 42
Disposal Cost ($1,000)	125	143	226	314	358
Tons per week Total	46,426	52,995	52,995	52,995	52,995
Tons per week to Meadowlands % of Total	40,294 87	46,004 87	43,962 83	39,743 75	28,576 54
Tons per week to Non-Meadowlands Landfills	6,132	6,991	9,003	13,252	24,419

[a] Meadowlands - Hackensack Meadowlands.

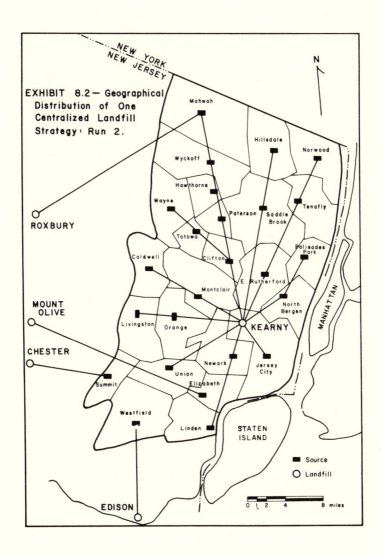

EXHIBIT 8.2— Geographical Distribution of One Centralized Landfill Strategy: Run 2.

low price ($2.70 per ton) charge in the Meadowlands results in the hauling of between 40,000 and 45,000 tons per week of solid waste to Meadowlands landfills.

Runs 3 to 5 pose the following question: How much can the disposal charge be raised before many waste sheds have a clear incentive to haul their waste to other landfill sites? This question is not academic because new landfill sites in the Meadowlands will be more expensive to operate, and the proposed baling operation or rail-haul would raise the disposal charge. Runs 3 to 5 were made with our first planning year data: 1980.

First, we raised the Meadowlands charge to $4.58 per ton, while maintaining the present charge at the other sites (Run 3). The optimization model made a negligible change in the hauling pattern. About 2,000 tons that had been allocated to the Meadowlands from the peripheral Linden (25) and Hillsdale (2) sheds were sent to other landfill sites. While only two additional waste sheds were given non-Meadowlands allocations, raising the charge from $2.70 to $4.58 per ton provides a clear economic incentive for six instead of only one waste shed not to haul to the Meadowlands. All of these waste sheds lie at the southern, southwestern, and northwestern extremes of the study area, are the furthest removed from the Meadowlands, and have relatively nearby disposal sites available in Middlesex or Morris counties.

Summarizing, at $4.58 per ton, more than four-fifths of the region's waste should come to the centralized Meadowlands landfills. It would appear that in the absence of new landfills the disposal charge in the Meadowlands could be raised to $4.58 per ton without much change in the region's waste-hauling pattern.

At $7 per ton, the estimated charge for a baling system, the waste of eight of the 25 waste sheds is allocated to non-Meadowlands landfills. In addition, 15 of the remaining 17 waste sheds have an economic incentive to haul to at least one of the other landfills. About half require transfer stations to justify these long hauls. Unfortunately the 13,000 tons per week from the eight other regional waste sheds uses up all the disposal capacity of the Morris County sites. Clearly, however, at $7 per ton in the Meadowlands, one should expect extremely strong pressures for the development of new landfills or other means of disposal from Bergen and Passaic County communities.

Finally, a $10 per-ton charge (equivalent to rail-haul) provides economic incentive for every waste shed to find an alternative to Meadowlands disposal. The Middlesex County landfills and Morris County landfills are allocated about 26,000 tons of waste per week (almost half the region's projected total).

In conclusion, the five-county region is likely to pay dearly for the continuation of the centralized landfilling strategy. At a modest $4.58-per-disposal charge, the disposal cost to the 25 waste sheds rises 20 percent ($80,000 per week) above the base price 1980 estimate. Yet, nearly all the communities will have to continue to haul to the Meadowlands because other less expensive alternatives do not currently exist. At $7 per ton, the price the Hackensack Meadowlands Commission has quoted for its proposed baling operation, the cost to the region rises 55 percent ($180,000 per week)! And yet, with the exception of spatially peripheral agencies, three-fourths of the waste is still allocated to the Meadowlands because of a lack of inexpensive alternatives. In short, at $7 per-ton disposal charges, enormous pressures are likely to be generated to develop alternatives to hauling to the Meadowlands for landfilling.

A DISPERSED, REGIONAL LANDFILL STRATEGY

In the face of substantially increased disposal charges in the Meadowlands, an obvious alternative is the development of regional landfill sites dispersed throughout the region. We made more than 20 model runs to determine where new regional landfill sites could be economically justified. Runs 6 to 9 summarize these efforts (Exhibit 8.3).

First, the Meadowlands price was raised from $2.70 to $4.58 per ton, and seven 2,000 (TPD) capacity landfills were located (Run 6). Only three of these sites survived economically: Saddle Brook at capacity; Hanover at 1,500 tons per day; and Mahwah at about 150 tons per day. The southern sites (Bridgewater and South Brunswick) are too far to attract any waste from the study area. Two western sites (Totowa and Fairfield) are caught between the proposed Saddle Brook and Hanover sites and therefore get considerably less than 2,000 tons per week.

The three sites which survive indicate that central Bergen County (Saddle Brook facility) and western Essex or eastern Morris County (Hanover facility) are excellent sites for new regional disposal facilities that could divert about 20,000 TPW from the Meadowlands. The small Mahwah facility survives only because of the combination of the increased disposal charge and the long haul (Exhibit 8.4).

EXHIBIT 8.3

ESTIMATED COSTS OF A DISPERSED LANDFILL STRATEGY
(All runs assume 1980 generation rates)

Model Results	Run Number 6	7	8	9
Meadowlands Cost $ Per ton	4.58	4.58	7.00	7.00
Total cost ($1,000)	395	406	401	445
Haul Cost ($1,000)	160	166	171	178
% of Total	41	41	43	40
Disposal Cost ($1,000)	235	240	230	267
Tons Per week, Total	52,995	52,995	52,995	52,995
Tons Per week to Meadowlands	23,340	31,768	0	8,663
% of Total	44	60	0	16
Tons Per Week to Non-Meadowlands Existing Landfills	9,033	9,033	9,033	11,257
Tons Per week, to Proposed Landfills	20,622	12,194	43,962	33,075
Proposed Landfills Size in Tons Per day [a]	SDB-2,000 HAN-1,500 MAH- 150	SDB-1,000 HAN-1,000 MAH- 150	SDB-2,000 HAN-2,000 TOT-2,000 FRF-1,500 MAH- 150	SDB-1,000 HAN-1,000 TOT-1,000 FRF-1,000 SBR-1,000 MAH- 500

[a] SDB - Saddle Brook; HAN - Hanover
   MAH - Mahwah; FRF - Fairfield
   TOT - Totawa; SBR - South Brunswick
   BRW - Bridgewater

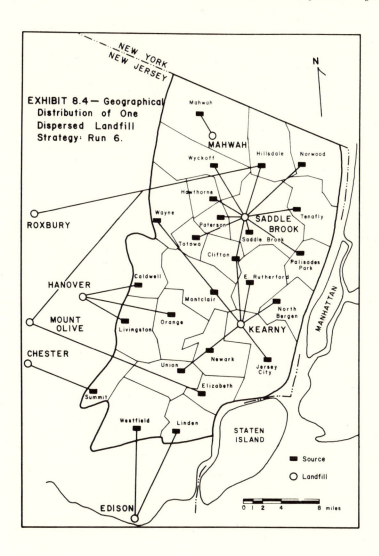

EXHIBIT 8.4— Geographical Distribution of One Dispersed Landfill Strategy: Run 6.

Both reducing the size of the proposed landfills to
1,000 TPD (Run 7) and running the model with projected
1985 waste-generation rates do not significantly change
the results. Indeed, the only change was an increase in
the regional system costs. The reduction of the proposed
landfill sites from 2,000 to 1,000 TPD raised the regional
price $10,000 per week (3 percent). More important, how-
ever, the $5.01 charge at the 1,000 TPD landfills increased
the flow of waste to the Meadowlands to more than 30,000
TPW. The three smaller dispersed sites were allocated
only 12,000 TPW, whereas the three larger dispersed sites
diverted 21,000 TPW from the Meadowlands.

The 1985 runs supported the 1980 results. The same
sites survived, but at higher costs because of the greater
waste load. Thus an increase in the Meadowlands landfill
price from $2.70 to $4.58 per ton justifies the development of two major landfill sites in central Bergen and in
either western Essex or eastern Morris counties. The economic advantage to the region as a whole in 1980 is between
4 and 7 percent ($30,000 to $20,000 per week). To some
waste sheds the economic difference exceeds 20 percent. The
advantage to the Meadowlands of the dispersed facilities
is the reduction of waste inputs from between 40,000 and
45,000 TPW to between 23,000 and 32,000 TPW. Overall, a
disposal charge of $4.58 per ton in the Meadowlands does
not seem to provide a sufficient incentive to warrant a
major change in the region's pattern of solid waste movement.

In the face of a $7 or $10 per ton cost in the Meadowlands which translates to 23 to 45 percent ($100,000 to
$200,000) more per week in disposal charges, and in the
absence of a resource recovery strategy, we expect that tre-
mendous pressure would be built up for dispersed landfill
sites. Run 8 demonstrates that given the choice between $7
per ton in the Meadowlads and $4,58 at dispersed landfill
sites, the carters are likely to take the cheaper disposal
charge. Three 2,000 TPD landfill sites are justified at
Saddle Brook, Totowa, and Hanover. One 1,500 TPD facility
survives at Fairfield, and the 150 TPD site in Mahwah is
justified. None of the waste goes to the Meadowlands.

Alternatively, the $7 disposal charge warrants five
1,000 TPD facilities and one 500 TPD (Run 9). The 1,000
TPD landfill option sites, however, are a more expensive
alternative than their 2,000 TPD counterparts because of the
increase per ton disposal charge ($5.01) for the facilities.
Again the $10-per-ton Meadowland charge and the 1985
waste-generation yield the same conclusion at still higher
prices.

Summarizing, if the price for landfilling in the Meadowlands rises to about $7 per ton, a strong economic incentive
would exist for a dispersed regional landfill strategy. At
that disposal charge in the meadowlands between two and four
large landfills are warranted in central Bergen, western
Essex, and eastern Morris counties. These landfills would
hold the fort against a possible increase in total landfill
cost of between 25 and 45 percent. At the same time, they
would precipitate monumental political struggles in the affected communities, and they do not take advantage of solid
waste as a possible source of revenue.

A RESOURCE RECOVERY
ALTERNATIVE: DRY FUEL

From an economic perspective, landfilling seems to be a
stable solid waste management strategy at best and a much
more expensive approach at worst. We therefore tested two
resource recovery technologies: dry fuel and gas pyrolysis.
In each case three factors were systematically varied:
(1) location of facilities -- centralized in the Meadowlands or dispersed; (2) size of recovery facility -- 2,000
or 3,000 TPD; and (3) revenue for recovered products -- high,
medium, low. All runs were made with 1980 projected waste-
generation rates.

In the case of dry fuel, 16 optimization runs were
made. The four most important are summarized in Exhibit
8.5.

Low Revenue for Recovered
Waste Products

We began by trying to model some of the worst possible
circumstances from the perspective of dry fuel technology.
Low price revenue for energy products was assumed, and
the Meadowlands was allowed to receive waste for landfilling
at $4.58 per ton. A single 2,000 TPD, dry fuel facility sur-
vived and lowered the regional waste treatment cost from
$424,000 (Run 3) to $408,000 per week (Run 10).

Second, we again stipulated the low price revenue
circumstances combined with the presence of dispersed regional landfill sites, but no landfilling in the Meadowlands. As in Run 10, a single, centralized facility of
about 2,000 TPD survived (Run 11). Other runs were made
with different variations of the same low-revenue theme.
For example, a run was made with a combination of dispersed
2,000-TPD facilities,   low revenues, and Meadowlands land-

EXHIBIT 8.5

ESTIMATED COSTS OF A DRY FUEL STRATEGY
(All runs assume 1980 generation rates)

Model Results	10	11	12	13	14	15	16	17
Meadowlands Cost $ Per Ton	4.58	X	4.58	7.00	4.58	4.58	4.58	4.58
Total Cost ($1,000)	408	385	384	386	178	-79	145	-112
Haul Cost ($1,000)	214	192	176	220	263	263	230	230
Disposal Cost ($1,000)	194	193	208	166	-85	-342	-85	-342
Tons Per Week Total	52,995	52,995	52,995	52,995	52,995	52,995	52,995	52,995
Tons Per week to Meadowlands Landfills from Waste Sheds	21,744	X	10,437	0	0	0	0	0
Total Per week to Meadowlands Existing Landfills	19,712	19,712	11,361	11,418	0	0	0	0
Tons Per week to Proposed Dry Fuel Plants	11,539	12,997	10,575	41,577	52,995	52,995	52,995	52,995
Tons Per week to Proposed Landfills	X	20,286	20,622	X	0	0	0	0
Tons Per Week to Meadowlands Landfills from Dry Fuel Plants	1,730	1,950	1,586	6,237	7,949	7,949	7,949	7,949

ESTIMATED COSTS OF A DRY FUEL STRATEGY
(All runs assume 1980 generation rates)

Model Results	10	11	12	13	14	15	16	17
Proposed landfills and size in tons per day	X	SDB-2,000 HAN-1,500 MAH-150	SDB-2,000 HAN-1,500 MAH-150	X	0	0	0	0
Proposed dry fuel plants and size in tons per day	LYE-2,000	KRN-2,000	NEW-2,000	NEW-2,000 LYE-2,000 SDB-2,000 ELZ-1,500	KRN-10,000	Same as 14	NEW-2,000 LYE-2,000 SDB-2,000 ELZ-2,000 JC-1,500	Same as 16
Weekly Dry Fuel Product received by electric generating stations	BER-3,873 KRN-3,050	MAR-1,123 KRN-3,050 ESS-3,625	HUD-2,720 ESS-3,625	HUD-7,171 MAR-332 KRN-3,959 ESS-3,625 LIN-4,866 BER-5,900	HUD-9,575 MAR-1,123 KRN-3,050 ESS-3,625 LIN-7,700 BER-5,900 SEW-597	Same as 14	Same as 14	Same as 14

SDB – Saddle Brook
HAN – Hanover
MAH – Mahwah
LYE – Lyndhurst
NEW – Newark
BER – Bergen
MAR – Marion
HUD – Hudson
SEW – Sewaren

FRF – Fairfield
SBR – South Brunswick
BRW – Bridgewater
KRN – Kearny (Meadowlands)
ELZ – Elizabeth
ESS – Essex
LIN – Linden

TOT – Totowa
JC – Jersey City

filling at $4.58 per ton. Run 12 indicated that even these
highly conservative assumptions justified a dry fuel plant
in Newark.

When the price for landfilling in the Meadowlands was
assumed to be raised from $4.58 to $7 per ton, three 2,000
TPD plants survived (in Newark, Lyndhurst, and Saddle Brook)
and one 1,500-TPD plant (in Elizabeth) (Run 13). Each
facility was allocated waste from adjacent communities. The
Saddle Brook facility was allocated waste from northern and
central Bergen and Passaic waste sheds. The Lyndhurst facility
received waste from southern Bergen, Hudson, northern Essex,
and Passaic counties. The Newark plant was allocated the
Newark solid waste and most of the western Essex county
waste. Finally, the Elizabeth facility received waste from
adjacent communities in Union County and western Essex counties.

Overall, these   low-revenue runs strongly argue that
authorities in the Meadowlands or in nearby communities such
as Newark should from an ecnomic perspective move toward
negotiating the development of a large dry fuel resource recovery facility. Even with an extremely modest revenue for
the recovered products, at least one major plant is justified. If low-priced, dispersed landfill sites are not provided elsewhere in or near the study area, then between two
and four dry fuel facilities are warranted.

Medium and High Revenue
For Recovered Products

While it is appropriate to analyze the survivability
of   a facility under the   low revenue conditions, the low
fuel cost assumption used in the previous section seems from
the mid-1970s perspective to be long-gone, like the five-
cent cigar and the twenty-cent hotdog. Therefore, we modeled the system assuming a revenue for No. 6 oil equivalent
to the late 1974 and early 1975 price per barrel (our high
price) and a price midway between the "low" and "high"
prices (our medium price).

The medium - and high - price simulations provide strong
arguments for a dry fuel alternative. First, we assumed
that the Meadowlands would through sets of 2,000 TPD plants
provide enough capacity to take the entire 1980 waste load
of the region (about five 2,000 TPD plants). We did not
assume that centralized dry fuel facility capacity would be
provided by huge 5,000 to 7,000 TPD plants. These facilities should theoretically lower the disposal charge because
of better economies of scale then 2,000 TPD plants. However, as yet they have not been demonstrated to be feasible

to our satisfaction from the economic or traffic perspectives.

Run 14 included a 55,000 TPW, dry fuel capacity in the Meadowlands, the availability of existing landfill capacity and the development of new, dispersed landfill sites by 1980. The model assigned all of the waste to the Meadowlands dry fuel facilities at a total weekly regional cost of $178,000 (Run 14). This regional cost is less than 60 percent of the estimated 1975 cost (Run 1 -- $298,000) and 42 percent of the estimated base price, 1980 cost (Run 3 -- $424,000).

When the revenue for the energy product was raised to current levels and the same set of assumptions were retained about Meadowlands capacity, the unthinkable happened -- a revenue was produced (Run 15). If, indeed, revenue of almost $80,000 per week was produced, the region would be in the comforting position of arguing whether the funds should be allocated to building parks in the Meadowlands, used to finance education, given back to the waste-shed communities, or used in numerous other activities. In short, we have found that depending upon the revenue for fuel at least one and perhaps five 2,000 TPD dry fuel plants are warranted in the Meadowlands or vicinity by as early as 1980.

The Meadowlands area organizations may not, however, be able or willing to raise the revenue for the facilities. In addition, opposition from local residents to the continued influx of all the regions waste may be high. Accordingly, we modeled the low, medium, and high revenue circumstances for dispersed, 2,000 TPD dry fuel plants.

Earlier we concluded that a single 2,000 TPD facility could survive in Newark even if faced with competition by Meadowlands landfills, with a $4.58 per ton disposal charge, and new, dispersed landfills (Run 12). When the Meadowlands price was increased to $7 per ton, three 2,000-TPD and one 1,500-TPD dispersed facility were justified.

The medium and best price, dispersed, dry fuel simulations were made with the following facility assumptions: (1) six 2,000 TPD dry fuel facilities located in Newark, Lyndhurst, Saddle Brook, Totowa, Jersey City, and Elizabeth; (2) available capacity in existing landfills and (3) available dispersed landfill capacity. The optimization and procedure allocated all of the waste to the dry fuel facilities at a weekly cost of $145,000 (Run 16). The $145,000 cost is less than half the estimated 1975 cost (Run 1 -- $298,000 and 34 percent of the estimated base

price, 1980 cost (Run 3 -- $424,000). In addition, the dis-
persed system cost was $33,000 per week (about 20 percent)
cheaper than the medium-revenue, centralized dry fuel system.
This $33,000-per-week advantage of the dispersed system
should be viewed as one indicator of the opportunity cost
of locating all the region's waste disposal capacity in the
Meadowlands. The geographical distribution of solid waste
movements for the dispersed dry fuel system is illustrated
by Exhibit 8.6. Most of the hauls are relatively short and
fall within the county in which the waste shed is located.

The same opportunity cost was obtained when the dispersed,
dry fuel system was modeled assuming current (our high)
energy price revenues. The model estimated a weekly revenue
of $112,000, which is $33,000 per week more than the $79,000
revenue generated by the centralized dry fuel alternative.

Overall, if the communities in the study area wish to
force the Meadowlands to absorb all of their solid waste,
then as a whole they will have to incur an additional $33,000
per week in transportation costs. Individual waste-shed and
community costs will, of course, vary depending upon the
length of the travel and the locations of facilities.

In conclusion, if reasonable contracts for dry fuel products can be negotiated with the utilities and if communities can be persuaded to continue consistently to bring
their waste to the Meadowlands, then the dry fuel option is,
from an economic perspective, clearly preferable to centralized or dispersed landfilling. If groups of communities,
probably county or large cities, choose to take the responsibility of waste disposal away from the Meadowlands, then the
cost to most of such communities will be further reduced.
The political costs of county or large-city management of
the final stage of solid waste disposal are uncalculatable
but probably unacceptably high in many areas.

GAS PYROLYSIS: A SECOND
RESOURCE RECOVERY ALTERNATIVE

Gas pyrolysis is a new and expensive technology. It
has been suggested that the gas product is more adaptable
to the region's utility boilers and to industrial uses than
is the dry fuel technology. Therefore, we tested gas pyrolysis as a possible alternative to the dry fuel technology.
Facility locations, plant capacity, and revenue for the
recovered products were varied in over a dozen optimization
runs. A centralized and a dispersed regional pattern were
examined. The recovery facilities were set at 2,000 and

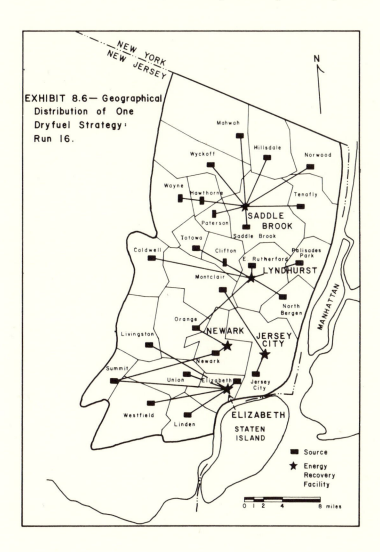

EXHIBIT 8.6— Geographical Distribution of One Dryfuel Strategy: Run 16.

EXHIBIT 8.7

ESTIMATED COSTS OF A GAS PYROLYSIS STRATEGY
(All runs assume 1980 generation rates)

Model Results	18	19	20	21	22	23	24	25
Total Cost ($1,000)	422	412	391	385	293	140	279	126
Haul Cost, ($1,000)	210	190	167	160	198	198	184	184
Disposal Cost ($1,000)	212	222	224	225	95	-58	95	-58
Tons Per week Total	52,995	52,995	52,995	52,995	52,995	52,995	52,995	52,995
Tons Per week to Non-Meadowlands Existing Landfills	19,712	13,158	19,712	13,158	0	0	923	0
Tons Per Week to Proposed Landfills	X	X	20,622	20,622	0	0	0	0
Tons Per week to Gas Pyrolysis Facilities	33,283	39,837	12,661	19,215	52,995	52,995	52,072	52,995
Proposed Landfills & Size in Tons Per Day a	X	X	SDB-2,000 HAN-1,500 MAH- 150	SDB-2,000 HAN-1,500 MAH- 150	0	0	0	0
Proposed Gas Pyrolysis Plants & Size in Tons Per day b	KRN-6,000	KRN-3,000 NEW-3,000 BER-1,500	KRN-2,000	KRN-1,500 NEW-2,000	KRN-10,000	Same as 22	KRN-4,500 NEW-3,000 BER-2,000	Same as 24

(continued)

EXHIBIT 8.7 (continued)

ESTIMATED COSTS OF A GAS PYROLYSIS STRATEGY
(All runs assume 1980 generation rates)

Model Results	18	19	20	21	22	23	24	25
Tons Per week of Energy Product received by Generating Stations[c]	KRN-26,626	KRN-12,889 ESS-13,281 BER- 5,698	KRN-10,128	KRN-6,912 NEW-8,460	KRN-42,396	Same as 22	KRN-20,000 NEW-13,843 BER- 7,814	KRN-20,000 NEW-13,843 BER- 8,552

[a]SDB - Saddle Brook: HAN - Hanover; MAH - Mahwah
[b]KRN - Kearny (Meadowlands); NEW - Newark; BER- Bergen
[c]Generating Stations: BER - Bergen; KRN - Kearny; ESS - Essex

3,000 TPD. And the revenue for the gas product was tested at high, medium, and low levels. All runs were made with 1980 projected waste-generation rates. The most important runs are summarized in Exhibit 8.7.

Low Revenue for Recovered Products

We began by determining if gas pyrolysis facilities could survive under low revenue conditions. First, low price revenue for energy products was assumed, none of the proposed dispersed landfills were permitted, and the Meadowlands was given enough gas pyrolysis capacity to absorb all of the region's waste in modular 3,000 TPD plants. The Meadowlands absorbed more than 30,000 TPW of waste products (Run 18). However, the regional cost ($422,000) was only $2,000 less per week than the estimated costs of continuing the centralized landfilling strategy (Run 3 -- $424,000).

Next, a dispersed gas pyrolysis system was studied under the conditions of no new dispersed regional landfills or no landfilling in the Meadowlands. Three facilities survived: Kearny at 3,000 TPD; Newark at 3,000 TPD; and Bergen at 1,500 TPD (Run 19).

When the gas pyrolysis system was placed in competition with the proposed dispersed landfills, the landfills were allocated nearly all the waste (Runs 20 and 21). One 2,000 TPD facility survived in the Meadowlands (Run 20) and two dispersed facilities were justified, one at 2,000 TPD and a second at 1500 TPD (Run 21).

Summarizing, gas pyrolysis technology does not fare well in competition with Meadowlands or with dispersed regional landfills at $4.58 per ton. If the price for disposal landfills in the Meadowlands rises to $7 per ton, then a large pyrolysis plant could survive under low revenue circumstances. While products from gas pyrolysis may be more acceptable to utilities than products from a dry fuel process, unless the utilities are willing to pay more than a minimum price for the gas, the facility may not be constructed.

Medium and High Revenue for Recovered Products

The picture for the gas pyrolysis technology is brighter if one can assume today's (high) revenue for the product or a revenue midway between "high" and "low" revenues. If

a medium revenue can be assumed, the regional weekly cost
is $293,000 (Run 22). This weekly cost is comparable to
the 1975 estimated regional cost (Run 1 -- $298,000) and
is 29 percent of the estimated 1980 base price cost (Run
3 -- $424,000). The high-price assumption produced a total
system cost of $140,000 per week, a price about half the
estimated 1975 cost (Run 23).

The dispersed facility runs (24 and 25) justified
4,500 TPD capacity in the Meadowlands, a 3,000 TPD facility
in Newark, and a 2,000 TPD plant in southern Bergen County.
In our study area, with the exceptions of the Linden and
Sewaren generating stations, all major utility stations are
located in and around the Hackensack Meadowlands. Even at
these higher revenue prices, the proposed Union County facility was not allocated enough waste to justify a 2,000
TPD facility. In reality, the geography of the dispersed
sites resembles that of the centralized pattern because
plants are restricted to sites near electric generating
stations (Run 24).

The differences between the regional costs for the
centralized and dispersed gas pyrolysis options under medi-
um-and high-price options are negligible. Therefore, total
cost would probably not be an important consideration in
the decision to choose or to reject a dispersed or centralized
gas pyrolysis technology. Gas pyrolysis is likely to be
accepted or rejected on the basis of its advantages and disadvantages in relation to other technologies.

The important distinctions between the dry fuel
and gas pyrolysis technologies favor the dry fuel system.
The dry fuel technology is much less expensive. It has a
longer operating record than the gas pyrolysis technology.
Dry fuel plants may compete economically at smaller sizes
and need not be located extremely close to utility generating stations. Accordingly, the pattern of hauls under the
dry fuel technology (Exhibit 8.6) are shorter than the
counterpart hauls under the gas pyrolysis strategy (Exhibit
8.8). Conversely, unlike dry fuel, the gas pyrolysis
technology should not leave a residue to be landfilled, and
the dry fuel technology may not be amenable to the boilers
of its potential market.

As a final comparative summary of all the systems
modeled in this study, Exhibit 8.9 compares the total waste
disposal charges for each waste shed in six of the most important optimization runs. Each disposal charge represents
the per-ton cost charged to the waste source during that
run. The six possible comparisons clearly demonstrate the
economic advantage of the dry fuel technology, whether

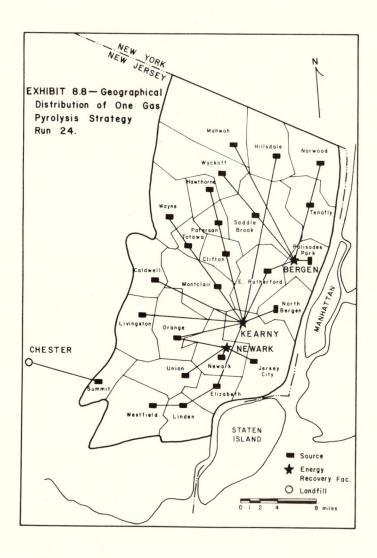

EXHIBIT 8.8— Geographical Distribution of One Gas Pyrolysis Strategy Run 24.

EXHIBIT 8.9

WASTE DISPOSAL COST TO WASTE SHEDS FOR SELECTED RUNS: DISPOSAL CHARGE AND TRANSPORTATION
(Cost in Dollars Per Ton)

Waste Shed	*Run Number*					
	(3) Central-ized Land-fill	*(6)* Dispersed Landfill	*(14)* Central-ized Dry Fuel	*(16)* Dispersed Dry Fuel	*(22)* Central-ized Gas Pyrolysis	*(24)* Dispersed Gas Pyrolysis
1	8.16	7.87	3.97	2.10	7.36	7.67
2	10.14	8.88	3.96	2.89	7.35	7.35
3	10.64	8.48	4.46	2.30	7.85	7.50
4	10.61	8.26	4.43	2.08	7.82	8.20
5	8.68	6.32	2.50	.14	5.89	5.79
6	10.20	8.05	4.02	1.87	7.41	6.51
7	7.21	7.21	1.03	.21	4.42	4.75
8	9.53	8.42	3.35	2.12	6.74	5.25
9	7.64	7.64	1.46	.68	4.85	4.85
10	8.86	8.86	2.68	.76	6.07	5.56
11	8.26	8.26	2.08	1.40	5.47	5.47
12	8.89	7.27	2.71	1.09	6.10	6.10
13	7.70	6.06	1.52	.12	4.91	4.91
14	7.53	6.80	1.35	.90	4.74	4.74
15	6.83	6.74	.65	.57	4.04	4.04
16	7.75	6.75	1.57	1.74	4.96	4.96
17	7.12	7.12	.94	1.35	4.33	4.33
18	8.97	6.43	2.79	3.72	6.18	6.18
19	7.77	7.39	1.59	2.14	4.98	4.94
20	8.08	8.08	1.90	1.99	5.29	4.21
21	6.89	6.89	3.18	2.95	6.57	6.89
22	7.64	7.64	1.46	.87	4.85	4.29
23	6.45	6.45	2.17	1.52	5.57	5.57
24	7.15	7.15	2.86	1.95	6.27	6.27
25	8.51	8.51	3.50	.65	6.89	6.89
Total Region	8.00	7.45	3.36	2.74	5.53	5.26
Total Region Cost, $1,000 per week [a]	424	395	178	145	293	279

[a]The total regional cost also includes the cost of moving the dry fuel product from the recovery facility to the utility station and the waste from the facility to the landfill. The 25 waste shed costs do not reflect these secondary links.

centralized (Run 14) or dispersed (Run 16). They also indicate the less convincing economic advantages of the gas
pyrolysis technology (22 and 24) over either of the landfilling options.

Neither the dispersed nor the centralized landfilling
strategies are economically competitive with the dry fuel
or gas pyrolysis technologies. From an economic perspective, the dry fuel technology is the preferred alternative.
It has clear economic advantages over any other system both
as a centralized system in the Meadowlands and at dispersed
sites. The 2,000 TPD facilities can either be clustered in
the Meadowlands or dispersed to sites in each of the counties.

Gas pyrolysis is preferable to centralized landfilling.
However, under the low revenue conditions, it suffers in
competition with a dispersed landfill strategy. Under medium - and high - price revenue circumstances it is clearly,
superior to centralized or dispersed landfilling. At the
present time it is restricted to sites near energy users,
a fact which in our study area limits its adaptability.